TEACHER RESOURCES
FOR PRACTICE AND SUPPORT
WITH ANSWER KEY

McGRAW-HILL

SCIENCE

MATTER AND ENERGY

McGraw-Hill School Division
New York Farmington

The TRPS Contains:	
Data Sheets for PE Activities (also in ***Science Journal***)	Explore Activities • Skill Builders • Quick Labs
Data Sheets for TE Activities (BLMs only)	Alternative Explore Activities
Reading Suppport (BLMs only)	Reading Study Guides • Study Aids • Summaries • Cloze Tests
Practice Worksheets (also in ***Science Practice Workbook***)	Topic Practices • Chapter Practices

Matter and Energy

Chapter: Matter

Chapter: Energy

McGraw-Hill School Division

A Division of The ***McGraw-Hill*** *Companies*

McGraw-Hill School Division
Two Penn Plaza
New York, New York 10121

Printed in the United States of America
ISBN 0-02-277631-1 / 3
2 3 4 5 6 7 8 9 024 04 03 02 01 00

Name ______________________________ EXPLORE ACTIVITY 1

Investigate Which Object Takes Up More Space

Hypothesize What will happen when you put different objects in a container of water? How might you test your ideas?

Write a **Hypothesis:**

____

____

Test which object takes up more space by placing different objects in a container of water.

Materials

- 12-oz. plastic cup half full of water
- markers (different colors)
- a piece of clay
- classroom objects

Procedures

1. **Measure** Find the level of the water. Use a marker to mark the level on the outside of the cup.
2. **Predict** What will happen to the level of the water when you place the piece of clay in the cup? Record your prediction.

   ____

3. **Observe** Place the clay in the cup. What happens? Use a different color marker to mark the new water level on the outside of the cup. Remove the clay.

   ____

4. **Predict** Look at the other objects. Which object will make the water level change the most when you put it in the cup? Record your prediction.

   ____

5. **Experiment** Place one object at a time in the cup. Mark the new water level for each object. Use a different color marker for each object.

Conclude and Apply

1. **Identify** What happened each time you placed an object in the cup? Why?

 ____

 ____

2. **Compare and Contrast** How did the different objects affect the water level? Why do you think this happened?

 ____

 ____

3. **Draw Conclusions** Which object takes up the most space? How do you know?

 ____

 ____

Going Further: Problem Solving

4. **Experiment** What do you think will happen to the water level in the cup if you change the shape of the clay?

 ____

 ____

Inquiry

Think of your own questions that you might like to test. Will a heavy object or a light object cause a greater change in the water level? Write your question, a way to test your question, and your results on a separate sheet of paper.

Does Weight Matter?

Materials

- 600-mL beaker
- water
- 3 regular golf balls and 3 plastic golf balls

Procedures

1. Fill the beaker about half way with water. Measure and record the amount of water.

   ____

2. Place the regular golf balls in the water. Record the level of the water. Remove the balls from the beaker.

   ____

3. Place the plastic balls in the water. Hold them just under the surface. Record the level of the water. Remove the balls from the beaker.

   ____

Conclude and Apply

1. Which type of golf ball is heavier? Which takes up more space?

   ____

   ____

2. Compare how high the water level rose with each type of ball. Explain your observations.

   ____

   ____

   ____

   ____

Rock, Clocks, Trees, and Bees

In this topic, you will learn how to identify objects by describing them.

Matter is anything that has mass and takes up space. Bricks, pencils, and soccer balls all have mass and take up space, so they are all matter.

Some objects take up more space than others. An object that takes up more space has a greater volume. **Volume** is how much space matter takes up. A refrigerator has a greater volume than a brick.

Another way to describe matter is to describe the matter's mass. **Mass** is how much matter is in an object. An object with a large mass feels heavy. An object with a small mass feels light. A school bus has more mass than a bike. A bike has more mass than an apple.

You can measure the mass of an object. One unit used to measure mass is the gram. One gram is a small amount of mass. Two paper clips equal about one gram. A nickel is about five grams. You can use the letter g to represent the word gram. You can measure the mass of larger things in kilograms. One kilogram is equal to 1,000 grams. You can represent the word kilogram with the letters kg.

When you describe an object, you are naming its properties. A **property** is a characteristic of something. Some properties are common to all types of objects. For example, all matter has volume and mass. Other properties are special to each type of matter. Size, shape, color, and texture are other properties of matter. Some objects are hard, while others are soft. Some objects float in water, while others sink.

Mass and weight are related. An object with more mass also has greater weight. The weight of an object is the pull of gravity on that object by Earth or any other large body in space. Gravity is the pulling force between two objects. Gravity is much stronger on Earth than on the Moon, because Earth has much more mass than the Moon.

Rocks, Clocks, Trees, and Bees

Fill in the blanks.

Which Object Takes Up More Space?

1. Since a brick and a pencil both take up space, they are both types of ______________.

2. The more space an object takes up, the greater its ______________.

3. Since a tennis ball takes up less space than a soccer ball, a tennis ball has less ______________ than a soccer ball.

4. The amount of matter that is in an object is called its ______________.

5. The mass of an apple is ______________ than the mass of a school bus.

6. Since the particles in a book are packed more tightly than the particles in a balloon, a book has more ______________ than a balloon.

How Do You Measure Mass?

7. The unit that is used to measure mass is a ______________.

8. Since a school bus is large, its mass is measured in ______________.

9. Since a paper clip is small, its mass is measured in ______________.

10. One kilogram is equal to ______________ grams.

Fill in the blanks.

How Else Can You Describe Matter?

11. A property is a(n) ________________ of an object.

12. Two properties of all matter are volume and ________________.

13. Size and shape are two ________________ of matter.

14. A property of a raft is that it ________________ in water.

How Are Mass and Weight Related?

15. The greater the mass of an object, the greater its ________________.

16. The weight of an object is the pull of ________________ on that object.

17. As the mass of two objects increases, the pull of gravity between the objects ________________.

18. As the distance between two objects increases, the pull of gravity between the objects ________________.

19. Since the Moon has less ________________ than Earth, the pull of gravity is weaker on the Moon than on Earth.

Measuring Mass

Hypothesize Do objects in your classroom have different masses?

Write a **Hypothesis:**

____

____

Materials

- balance
- small objects
- 30 paper clips

Procedures

1. Estimate the mass of each object. Record your estimates.

   ____

   ____

2. **Measure** Measure the mass of each object. Place the object on one side of the balance. Place paper clips on the other side until the two sides balance. Record the number of paper clips used to balance each object in the table below.

3. **Use Numbers** What is the mass of each object? (Remember, two paper clips equals about one gram.) Record the mass of each object in the table.

Object	Number of Paper Clips	Mass of Object

Conclude and Apply

1. **Compare and Contrast** How does your list of estimated masses compare with the measurements you recorded?

____

2. **Plan** If you wanted to find the mass of your shoe, how could you do it? How many paper clips would you need?

____

____

Going Further A nickel equals about 5 grams. How can you use nickels to find the mass of objects in your classroom? Write and conduct an experiment.

My Hypothesis Is:

____

____

____

My Experiment Is:

____

____

____

____

My Results Are:

____

____

____

Rocks, Clocks, Trees, and Bees

A diagram uses pictures and words to describe a thing or a process. This diagram shows a boy and a cat on Earth, on the Moon, and on Jupiter. The labels tell you that the diagram has information about the weight and mass of the boy and the cat. Use the diagram to answer the following questions.

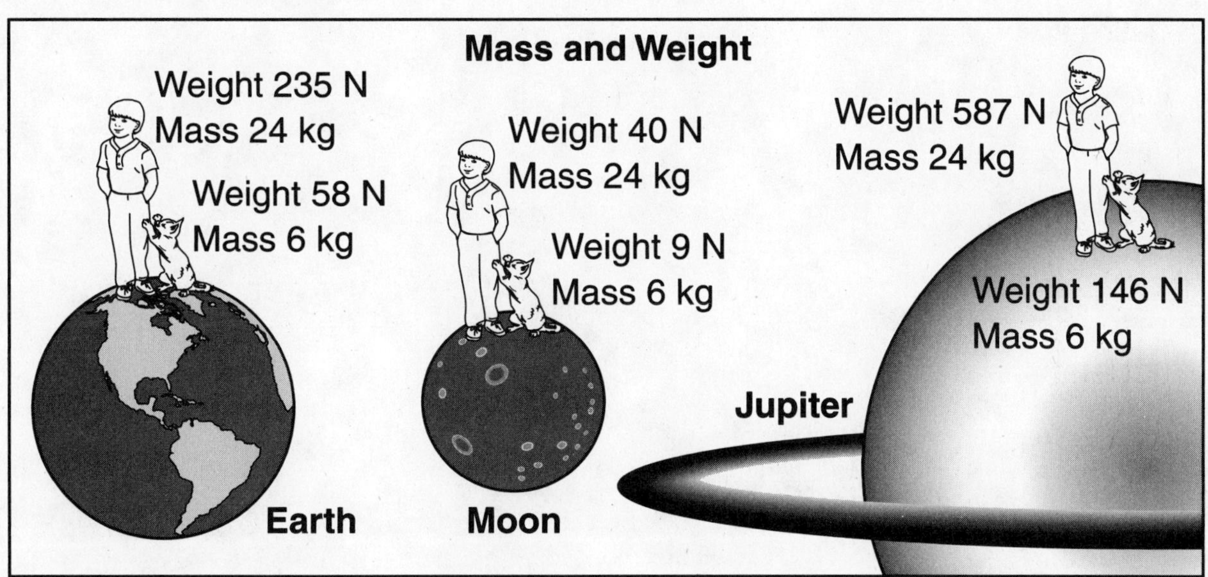

1. What is the weight of the boy on Earth? On the Moon? On Jupiter?

____

2. What is the mass of the boy on Earth? On the Moon? On Jupiter?

____

3. What is the weight of the cat on Earth? On the Moon? On Jupiter?

____

4. What is the mass of the cat on Earth? On the Moon? On Jupiter?

____

5. Look at the weight of the boy and the weight of the cat in each location. Do you see a pattern? List the locations in order from where the weight is the least to where it is greatest.

____

6. What do you notice about the mass of the boy and the mass of the cat in each location?

____

____

Name ____ CLOZE TEST 1

Rocks, Clocks, Trees, and Bees

Fill in the blanks.

You can describe an object by naming a(n) ________________, or characteristic, of the object. All matter has ________________ and ________________. Other properties are special for each type of matter, for example, size, shape, color, and ________________. There are more properties you can use to describe matter. For example, some objects float in water and other objects ________________.

Rocks, Clocks, Trees, and Bees

Use one of these words to complete sentences 1–6.

gravity	space	properties
matter	particles	volume

1. The amount of space an object takes up is called its ____________.

2. Mass is a measure of how much ____________ an object contains.

3. The weight of an object is the pull of ____________ on the object.

4. All matter is made up of ____________.

5. Matter is anything that takes up ____________ and has mass.

6. You can describe matter by naming its ____________.

Answer these questions in your own words.

7. You have one bag of trash with a mass of 3 kg and another bag of trash with a mass of 14 kg. What do you know about the weights of the bags of trash?

____

____

8. You have a bowl of pancake batter. You add a quart of blueberries to the batter. What happens to the level of the batter in the bowl when you add the blueberries?

____

9. A dog weighs 70 N on Earth. If the dog is sent to the Moon, how would its weight change? How would its mass change?

____

____

Name ______________________________

Design Your Own Experiment

How Can You Classify Matter?

Hypothesize How can you tell whether a material is a solid or a liquid? How might you test your ideas?

Write a **Hypothesis:**

____

____

____

Materials

- plastic container of Oobleck
- investigation tools
- newspaper
- safety goggles

Procedures **Safety** Wear goggles.

1. **Observe** Observe the Oobleck using only your senses. How does the Oobleck look? What does it feel like? Record all of your observations.

   ____

   ____

2. **Experiment** Using the tools given to you, investigate the Oobleck in different ways. What new things do you observe? Record these observations.

   ____

   ____

3. **Classify** Look at the observations of Oobleck that you have made. Then review the definitions of solid and liquid that you wrote. Do you think Oobleck is a solid or a liquid? Could it be both? Why?

   ____

   ____

Conclude and Apply

1. **Communicate** What observations did you make about the properties of Oobleck?

____

____

2. **Explain** How did you decide to classify Oobleck? What observations helped you make your decision?

____

____

Going Further: Problem Solving

3. **Hypothesize** What do you think Oobleck is made of? How might you find out whether your idea is correct?

____

____

Inquiry

Think of your own questions that you might like to test. What else can you find out about Oobleck?

My Question Is:

____

How I Can Test It:

____

My Results Are:

____

____

Changing Forms

Materials

- ice cubes
- cups of water

Procedures

1. Observe the ice and water. Record their properties.

   ____

2. Decide what type of matter the ice and water are, and explain your decision.

   ____

   ____

3. Think of a way that you could change the ice into water. Write your plan on a separate sheet of paper. Show your plan to your teacher. Once your teacher has approved your plan, try it. Observe and record your results.

   ____

   ____

Conclude and Apply

1. How did the properties of the ice change when you tried your plan?

   ____

   ____

2. How can you tell when something is a solid? A liquid?

   ____

   ____

Comparing Solids, Liquids, and Gases

In this topic you will learn about three forms of matter—solids, liquids, and gases.

Three forms of matter are solids, liquids, and gases. Each form of matter takes up space and has mass. A **solid** is matter that has a definite shape and volume. Definite means that it stays the same. If you put a sneaker in a container, it stays the same shape in the container as it had outside the container. Its volume stays the same, too. In a solid, the particles of matter are packed closely together. They form a certain pattern which gives the solid its definite shape.

Juice is an example of a liquid. A **liquid** is matter that has a definite volume, but not a definite shape. A liquid takes the shape of the container it is in. The particles in a liquid are close together but do not form a certain pattern. Particles in a liquid have more energy than particles in a solid. Particles in a liquid are able to slide past one another. That is why liquids change their shape.

Another form of matter is gas. A **gas** is matter that has no definite shape or volume. The particles in a gas spread out to fill a large container or squeeze together to fit into a smaller container. Gases take the shape of the container they are in. Air is made of gases.

Matter can change and still be the same type of matter. When you slice an orange, the orange may look different, but it is made from the same particles as before it was cut. Matter can also change form and still be the same type of matter. You can find water in the form of a solid, a liquid, or a gas.

When you mix different types of matter together, you may get a **mixture.** In a mixture, each part has the same properties in the mixture that it has outside the mixture. Air is a mixture of gases. Salad dressing is a mixture of oil and vinegar. One special type of mixture is a **solution.** A solution is formed when one or more types of matter are spread evenly throughout another kind of matter.

Name ________________________________

Comparing Solids, Liquids, and Gases

Fill in the blanks.

How Can You Classify Matter?

1. Solids, liquids, and gases are alike in that they all take up space and have ________________.

2. All solids have a definite shape and ________________.

3. All liquids have a(n) ________________ volume.

4. A liquid does not have a definite ________________.

5. Since milk takes the shape of the container it is in, it is a(n) ________________.

6. A gas has no definite shape or ________________.

7. Both a gas and a(n) ________________ take the shape of the container they are in.

8. All solids, liquids, and gases are made of ________________.

9. The particles in a solid form a certain ________________.

10. The particles in a liquid have more ________________ than the particles in a solid.

11. The particles in a gas have more energy than the particles in a solid or a ________________.

12. The particles in a(n) ________________ can spread out to fill a large container or squeeze together to fit a small container.

Fill in the blanks.

How Can Matter Change?

13. Matter can change form and still be the same type of ________________.

14. Ice becomes liquid water when it ________________.

15. Water that evaporates changes from a liquid to a(n) ________________.

16. Particles in water vapor have more ________________ than the particles in solid or liquid water.

Can You Mix Different Kinds of Matter Together?

17. A mixture is a combination of different forms of ________________.

18. The properties of each type of matter in a(n) ________________ do not change.

What Is a Different Kind of Mixture?

19. When one or more types of matter are spread evenly throughout another type of matter, a ________________ is formed.

20. Salt water is a type of ________________.

Name ____

Comparing Solids, Liquids, and Gases

A diagram uses pictures and words to describe a thing or a process. This diagram shows particles in different forms of matter.

Particles in Different Forms of Matter

Solid

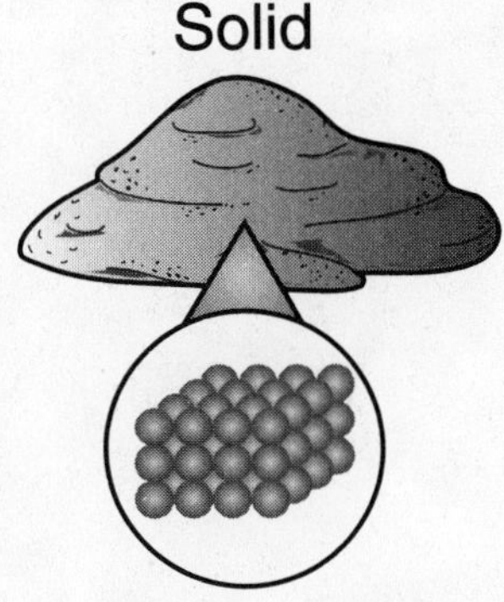

Liquid

Gas

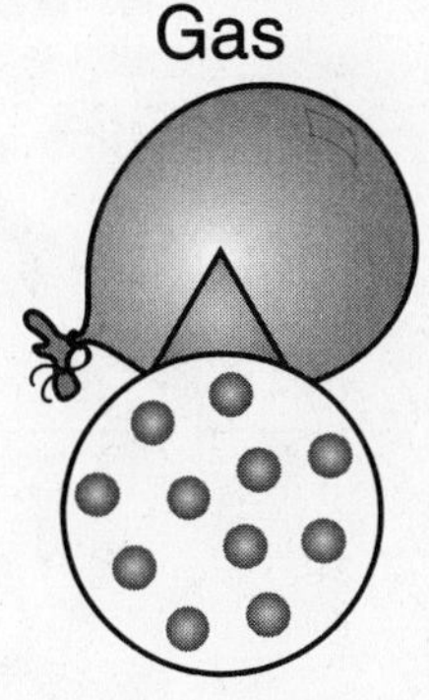

Use the diagram to answer the following questions.

1. What is the title of this diagram?

____

2. What forms of matter are shown in the diagram?

____

3. What do the close-ups show?

____

____

4. In which form of matter are the particles packed tightly together?

____

5. Which form of matter has the most space between its particles?

____

6. Describe the particles that make up a liquid.

____

____

Communicating

Making a Table

When you communicate you share information with others. Scientists communicate what they learn from an experiment. They might tell people how they think new information can be used. You can communicate by talking, or by creating a drawing, chart, table, or graph.

You can communicate what you know about the properties of solids, liquids, and gases. Look at the drawing on this page to help you answer the questions below.

Procedures

1. **Observe** Look at the drawing. What forms of matter do you see? What properties do these forms have? Record your observations.

____

____

____

____

____

2. Communicate Use your observations to fill in the table.

Forms of Matter	Properties

Conclude and Apply

1. Draw Conclusions What do solids and liquids have in common? What makes them different?

____

____

____

2. Communicate Give an example of a solid, a liquid, and a gas. Then write a sentence that tells what you know about the shape and volume of each one.

____

____

____

____

____

Name ____ CLOZE TEST 2

Comparing Solids, Liquids, and Gases

Fill in the blanks.

When water changes to a solid form, it is called ________________. As ice melts, it changes from a solid into a(n) ________________. The particles in water have more energy than the particles in ice. If water is warmed, it ________________ and changes into a gas. This gas is called water ________________. The particles in water vapor have more ________________ than the particles in water.

Comparing Solids, Liquids, and Gases

Use one of these words to complete sentences 1–7.

solid	volume	mixture	shape
gas	solution	energy	

1. Liquids have no definite ________________.
2. The particles in a gas have more ________________ than the particles in a solid.
3. The form of matter that can change volume is ________________.
4. Ice is the ________________ form of water.
5. Vegetable soup is a(n) ________________.
6. A solid has a definite shape and ________________.
7. Chocolate milk is a(n) ________________.

Answer these questions in your own words.

8. Can all three forms of matter exist in a mixture? If so, give an example of such a mixture.

____

____

____

9. You can shape a certain type of material just as if it were clay. Left alone at room temperature, the material forms a puddle. What form of matter is the material? Why?

____

____

____

Investigate What Magnets Attract

Hypothesize What kinds of items will be attracted to a magnet?

Write a **Hypothesis:**

____

____

Materials

- magnet
- several objects

Procedures

1. **Observe** Look at your objects. What properties of the objects do you observe? Record your observations.

   ____

2. **Predict** Which of the objects will be attracted to a magnet?

   Record your predictions. ______________________________

   ____

3. **Experiment** Test your predictions. Get a magnet from your teacher. Test each object to see if it is attracted to the magnet. Record the result of each test.

   ____

   ____

Conclude and Apply

1. **Classify** Look at the results of your tests. Which objects were attracted to the magnet? Which objects were not? Make two lists on a separate sheet of paper. In one list, write the names of the objects attracted to the magnet. In the other list, write those that were not. Title each of the lists.

2. Compare and Contrast Read the list of objects that were attracted to the magnet. Can you identify any properties that they all have in common? Write down your thoughts. Now look at the list of objects that were not attracted to the magnet. What kinds of things can you say about these objects? Write down your thoughts.

____

____

Going Further: Apply

3. What conclusions can you draw about the kinds of things that are attracted to magnets?

____

____

____

Inquiry

Think of your own questions that you might like to test. Can a magnet be used to separate objects?

My Question Is:

____

How I Can Test It:

____

____

My Results Are:

____

Name ________________________________

Treasure Hunt

Materials

- small objects
- large, deep pan of sand
- magnet

Procedures

1. Observe the objects. Predict whether or not you will be able to find each object using a magnet when the objects are buried in sand. Record your predictions.

____

____

____

____

2. Bury the objects in the sand.

3. Using only the magnet, locate as many buried objects as you can. Record the objects that you find.

____

____

Conclude and Apply

1. Which objects did you find with the magnet? Why were you able to find some objects with the magnet but not all?

____

____

2. Compare the objects you found with the magnet. How are they alike?

____

____

Building Blocks of Matter

In this topic you will learn about how the world is made up of the same basic building blocks.

Some objects are attracted to magnets. Other objects are not. Magnets attract some items made of metal. A **metal** is a shiny material found in the ground. Many of the items that magnets attract are made from the metals iron and steel. Magnets attract objects made from some other metals, too. Objects made from iron and steel have the property of magnetism. **Magnetism** is the property of an object that makes it attract iron and some other metals. Natural magnets come from a rock called magnetite. Magnetite is not a very strong magnet. Permanent magnets, made from iron and steel, are usually stronger than magnetite.

Iron is a very useful metal. It is mixed with other materials to make steel. Steel is a metal used to build buildings, railroads, and bridges. Your body uses iron in foods like meat and spinach to help keep healthy.

The metals iron, gold, silver, aluminum, and copper are elements. An **element** is a building block of matter. There are over 100 different elements. Some elements, like the metals iron and copper, are solids. Some elements are liquids. Some elements, like helium, are gases. Each element has its own special properties.

All elements are made up of **atoms.** An atom is the smallest particle of matter. The atoms that make up one element are all alike. They are different from the atoms that make up any other element.

When you combine the elements iron and oxygen you get a compound called rust. A **compound** may form when two or more elements are put together. The compound salt is made up of the elements sodium and chlorine. Water is a compound too. It is made of the elements hydrogen and oxygen. Remember that when a mixture is formed, different types of matter are mixed together. The properties of the matter in the mixture are not changed. However, the properties of a compound are different from the properties of the elements that make it up.

Building Blocks of Matter

Fill in the blanks.

What Do Magnets Attract?

1. Magnets attract items that are made of some types of ________________.
2. A magnet will ________________ a metal spoon.
3. Objects that are made from iron and steel have the property of ________________.
4. Magnetism is the property of an object that makes it attract ________________ and some other metals.
5. Junkyards use the property of magnetism to lift and sort objects made of ________________.
6. Natural magnets come from a rock called ________________.
7. Magnetite is not as strong as a(n) ________________ magnet.

What Are Some Other Uses of Iron and Steel?

8. Iron is mixed with other materials to make metals with different ________________.
9. Steel is a metal that is made from ________________.
10. You get iron from meats and dark green ________________.
11. You get iron from fortified ________________.

Fill in the blanks.

What Are Some Other Metals?

12. Gold, silver, aluminum, and copper are all types of ______________.

13. Each metal has its own special ______________.

14. ______________ is a heavy, hard metal.

15. Copper and ______________ are two light, soft metals.

16. Iron and gold are both ______________, or building blocks of matter.

17. An element can be a solid, liquid, or ______________.

18. A(n) ______________ is the smallest particle of matter.

How Can You Put Elements Together?

19. Iron and oxygen form a(n) ______________ called rust.

20. The properties of a compound are different from the properties of the ______________ that make it up.

Bowl of Iron

Hypothesize If you read the label on a box of breakfast cereal, you'll probably see iron in the list of ingredients. Does breakfast cereal really contain iron?

Write a **Hypothesis:**

____

____

Materials

- 1 package fortified cereal
- plastic sandwich bag
- magnet
- sheet of white paper

Procedures

1. Pour the cereal into a plastic bag. Add the magnet and seal the bag.
2. Shake the bag for several minutes. Carefully remove the magnet. Hold it over a sheet of white paper.
3. **Observe** What do you see when you look at the magnet?

____

____

Conclude and Apply

Predict What would happen if you tried the same experiment using cereal that did not contain iron?

____

____

Going Further Do different breakfast cereals contain different amounts of iron? How can you compare the amount of iron in different cereals? Write and conduct an experiment.

My Hypothesis Is:

____

____

____

My Experiment Is:

____

____

____

____

My Results Are:

____

____

____

____

Building Blocks of Matter: Metals

A chart is a way to organize information. This chart contains information about the properties of different metals.

Properties of Different Metals

① Steel is a very strong metal. Try digging a hole without a steel shovel!

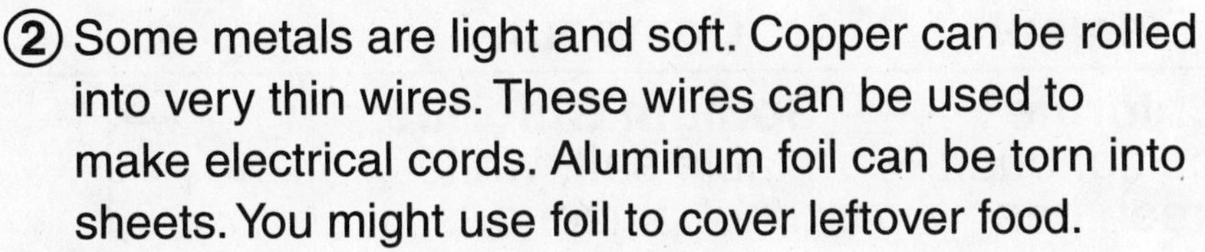

② Some metals are light and soft. Copper can be rolled into very thin wires. These wires can be used to make electrical cords. Aluminum foil can be torn into sheets. You might use foil to cover leftover food.

③ Some metals are very valuable. Gold and silver can be used to make beautiful jewelry.

Use the chart to answer the following questions.

1. What metals are described in the chart?

____

____

2. Which metal is very strong?

____

3. Which metal can be torn into sheets?

____

4. Which metals are used to make jewelry?

____

5. Name something that is made from steel.

____

6. Name something that is made from copper.

____

7. Contrast the types of metals described in each part of the chart.

____

____

____

Building Blocks of Matter: Compounds

A chart is a way to organize information. This chart contains information about common compounds. Each row describes a different compound. The top line in each row names the elements and the compound that they form. The bottom line in each row names properties of the elements and the compound.

COMMON COMPOUNDS					
Element		**Element**		**Compound**	
Sodium a soft metal	+	**Chlorine** a poisonous green gas	=	**Sodium Chloride** table salt, white not poisonous	
Hydrogen a gas that is lighter than air	+	**Oxygen** a gas	=	**Water** a liquid that is 1,000 times heavier than air	
Iron a hard metal	+	**Oxygen** a gas	=	**Rust** a soft, reddish crust	

Use the chart to answer the following questions.

1. What compound is described in the first row?

   ____

2. What compound is described in the last row?

   ____

3. What poisonous green gas is an element that forms sodium chloride?

   ____

4. What two elements make water?

   ____

5. What hard metal is an element that forms rust?

   ____

6. What compound is used as table salt?

   ____

7. Describe hydrogen.

   ____

Name ____ CLOZE TEST 3

Building Blocks of Matter

Fill in the blanks.

Magnets attract objects made of some types of ________________. A metal is a shiny material that can be found in the ________________. Many of the objects that magnets attract are made from the metals iron and ________________. Objects made from iron and steel have the property of ________________. The property of magnetism can be used to identify objects. Junkyards use powerful ________________ to lift and sort objects made of metal.

Name ____________________

Building Blocks of Matter

Use one of these words to complete sentences 1–8.

iron	matter	atoms	ground
elements	metal	aluminum	compound

1. If an object is attracted to a magnet, it must be made of ____________.
2. Metals are found in the ____________.
3. Steel is a metal that is made with ____________.
4. Elements are the building blocks of ____________.
5. All elements are made of ____________.
6. If the properties of elements change when they are mixed together, the mixture is called a(n) ____________.
7. One metal that is light and soft is ____________.
8. Your body contains about 11 different ____________.

Answer these questions in your own words.

9. Which elements are found in water? How is the compound different from its elements?

____

____

____

10. How can magnets be used for work?

____

____

Matter

Circle the letter of the best answer.

1. A gram is a unit that is used to measure

a. length. **b.** speed.

c. mass. **d.** weight.

2. Matter is

a. anything that you can see.

b. anything that takes up space and has mass.

c. anything that you can touch.

d. anything that has color.

3. Particles in a liquid have less energy than particles in

a. water. **b.** a computer.

c. ice. **d.** a gas.

4. Air is a mixture of different

a. liquids. **b.** solids.

c. gases. **d.** smells.

5. When one kind of matter is spread evenly throughout another type of matter, it is in a(n)

a. solution. **b.** mixture.

c. element. **d.** metal.

6. Everything in the world is made up of

a. water. **b.** elements.

c. vitamins and minerals. **d.** metals.

Circle the letter of the best answer.

7. Matter that has a definite volume but not a definite shape is called a(n)

a. solid. **b.** element.
c. liquid. **d.** gas.

8. Which of these is NOT a property of matter?

a. an opinion **b.** size
c. color **d.** shape

9. The amount of space that an object takes up is called its

a. size. **b.** shape.
c. weight. **d.** volume.

10. Blending different types of matter together makes a(n)

a. metal. **b.** mixture.
c. atom. **d.** element.

11. When different elements are blended to make a new material, such as sodium and chlorine combining to make salt, the result is called a

a. new element. **b.** metal.
c. compound. **d.** mixture.

12. Gold and silver are both

a. compounds. **b.** mixtures.
c. metals. **d.** liquids.

Name ______________________________

Investigate How Heat Affects Different Materials

Hypothesize You could measure how hot soil and water get when they are exposed to the same amount of heat. Would one type of matter warm up more than the other? How might you test your ideas?

Write a **Hypothesis:** ______________________________

____

____

Materials

- soil
- water
- 2 foam cups
- 2 thermometers
- heat source (sunlight or lamp)

Procedures

1. Fill one of the cups with water. Place an equal amount of soil in the other cup.
2. **Measure** Using your thermometers, measure how warm the soil and water are. Record your measurements.

   ____
3. Estimate how hot the soil and water will get if they are left in a warm place for 15 minutes. Record your estimates, then place the soil and water near a heat source. Make sure they are the same distance from the heat source.

   ____
4. **Measure** Record the readings on the thermometers every 5 minutes for 15 minutes. ______________________________
5. **Use Numbers** Find the difference between the first thermometer reading and the last. To do this, subtract the first measurement you made from the last measurement you made.

   ____

Conclude and Apply

1. **Identify** Which type of matter warmed up more? How do you know?

2. **Compare and Contrast** Were your estimates close to your actual measurements?

Going Further: Apply

3. **Infer** Why is it important to place the soil and water an equal distance from the heat source?

Inquiry

Think of your own questions that you might test. Which would get hotter when they are exposed to the same amount of heat—sand or water?

My Question Is:

How I Can Test It:

My Results Are:

Black and White

Materials

- black paper
- white paper
- two thermometers

Procedures

1. Cover one thermometer with black paper. Cover the other thermometer with white paper.
2. Place the thermometers in a sunny spot or under a lamp.
3. Predict which thermometer will have a higher reading after 5 minutes. Record your prediction.

   ____

   ____

4. Wait 5 minutes. Observe and record the thermometer readings.

   ____

   ____

Conclude and Apply

1. Which thermometer had a higher reading? Explain why.

   ____

   ____

2. What colors would be more comfortable to wear in hot weather? In cold weather?

   ____

   ____

Heat

In this topic you will learn about heat and how it affects matter.

Heat affects different types of matter differently. With the same amount of heat, one type of matter may warm up more than another type of matter. You can measure how much each type of matter warms up by using a thermometer.

Thermometers are used to measure temperature. **Temperature** is a measure of how hot or cold something is. Temperature is measured in degrees. A **degree** is the unit of measurement for temperature. The symbol for degree is °. **Heat** is a form of energy that makes things warmer. Heat can be added to a material to raise the material's temperature. Some materials need more energy to cause the same change in their temperature than others. It takes more energy to heat water than it takes to heat soil to the same temperature.

A thermometer is a glass tube filled with a liquid. When a thermometer is in a warm place, the liquid in the thermometer rises. It rises because the liquid expands when it is heated. Matter that expands gets bigger. It takes up more space.

When heat is added to matter, the particles in the matter move faster. As the particles move faster, they move farther apart. This movement makes matter expand.

Heat moves quickly through some types of matter. For example, some metals are used to make cooking pots. Heat moves quickly from the stove to the metal. The pot gets warm. Heat does not pass quickly through other materials. These materials are called insulators. An **insulator** is a material that heat does not travel through easily. Some materials, like wool, cotton, and air, are good insulators.

Heat

Fill in the blanks.

How Does Heat Affect Different Materials?

1. Heat affects different types of ______________ in different ways.

2. You can measure how much matter warms up by using a(n) ______________.

3. Thermometers measure ______________, which is how hot or cold an object is.

4. The unit of measurement for temperature is the ______________.

5. Energy makes ______________ move or change.

6. A form of energy that makes matter warmer is ______________.

7. Heat can be added to an object to raise the object's ______________.

8. It takes more energy to heat water than to heat soil to the same ______________.

9. The diagram shows that heat always flows from ______________ objects to cooler ones.

10. In the diagram, heat flowed from the warm air to the cold ______________.

11. In the diagram, heat flowed from the hot liquid to the boy's cold ______________.

Fill in the blanks.

How Does Heat Change Matter?

12. Heat is a form of ________________.

13. When a thermometer is in a warm place, the ________________ inside it expands.

14. Heat causes the particles in ________________ to move faster.

15. When matter loses ________________, its particles slow down.

16. As matter contracts, it takes up ________________ space.

How Can You Control the Flow of Heat?

17. Heat moves quickly through many ________________.

18. An insulator is a material that ________________ doesn't travel through easily.

19. Wool and cotton are both good ________________.

Name ____

Heat

A diagram uses pictures and words to describe a thing or a process. This diagram shows how heat moves. The arrows show the direction in which heat moves. Use the diagram to answer the following questions.

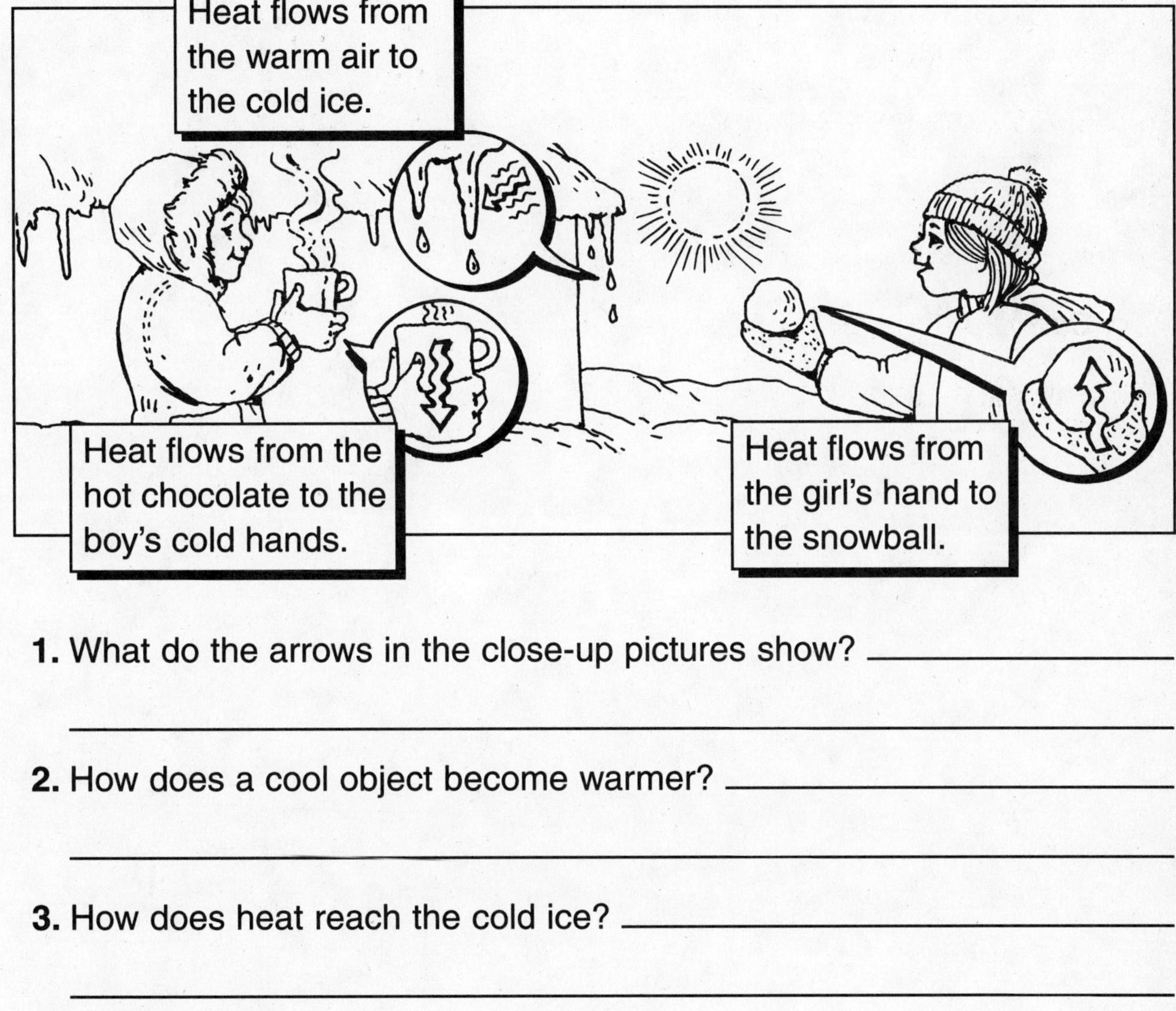

1. What do the arrows in the close-up pictures show? ____________________

____

2. How does a cool object become warmer? ____________________

____

3. How does heat reach the cold ice? ____________________

____

4. How does heat reach the boy's hands? ____________________

____

5. How does heat reach the snowball? ____________________

____

Expand and Contract

Hypothesize Do gases expand when heated? Do they contract when cooled?

Write a **Hypothesis:**

____

____

Materials

- balloon
- 2L plastic bottle
- bucket of warm water
- bucket of cool water

Procedures

1. Stretch the opening of the balloon over the opening of the bottle.
2. **Predict** What will happen when you place the bottle in the bucket of warm water? Test your prediction.

   ____

   ____

   ____

   ____

3. **Predict** What will happen when you place the bottle in the bucket of cool water? Test your prediction.

   ____

   ____

   ____

   ____

Name ______________________________________ QUICK LAB 4

Expand and Contract Page 2

Conclude and Apply

1. **Communicate** What happened to the balloon when you placed it in warm water? In cold water?

____

____

____

2. **Draw Conclusions** What happened to the air particles in the balloon when the bottle was in the warm water? The cool water?

____

____

____

Going Further Does the size of the bottle affect how the balloon expands? Write and conduct an experiment.

My Hypothesis Is:

____

My Experiment Is:

____

____

My Results Are:

____

____

Name ______________________________ CLOZE TEST 4

Heat

Fill in the blanks.

Temperature measures how ______________ or ______________ something is. Temperature can be measured by a(n) ______________. It is measured in ______________. The symbol for degree is °. A form of energy that makes matter warmer is ______________. Heat can be added to an object to raise the object's ______________. Some materials need more ______________ to raise their temperature than others.

Heat

Use one of these words to complete sentences 1–7.

thermometer	contracts	energy	temperature
degrees	insulators	expands	

1. The ________________ of an object is a measure of how hot or cold that object is.
2. Matter ________________ when it is heated.
3. It takes more ________________ to heat water than it takes to heat soil.
4. You can use a(n) ________________ to measure temperature.
5. Metals are generally not very good ________________ because heat flows through them quickly.
6. When matter is cooled, it ________________,or gets smaller.
7. Temperature is measured in units called ________________.

Answer these questions in your own words.

8. You are going on a camping trip to the North Pole. What materials would you use to make your tent in order to stay warm?

____

____

____

9. An egg is placed in a frying pan. The frying pan is then placed on the stove. How is heat transferred from the stove?

____

____

Name ______________________________ EXPLORE ACTIVITY 5

Investigate What Materials Light Passes Through

Hypothesize What kinds of materials can light pass through? How might you test your ideas?

Write a **Hypothesis:**

____

Test these materials to see which ones allow light to pass through.

Materials

- flashlight
- large balloon
- classroom materials

Procedures

1. **Experiment** Hold one material at a time in front of the lighted flashlight. Does the light shine through the material? Record your observations.

   ____

   ____

2. **Observe** Blow up your balloon. Look through the balloon. What do you observe now?

   ____

3. **Experiment** Try changing the other materials in some way. You may want to fold the papers several times to make them thicker, or crumple up the plastic wrap. After you have made a change in the material, test the material again. Record both the change you made and any new observations.

   ____

   ____

   ____

   ____

Conclude and Apply

1. **Classify** Which materials did the light pass through? List them. Which materials blocked the light? Make a separate list of the materials.

____

____

2. **Explain** What was the effect of the change you made to each material?

____

____

____

Going Further: Apply

3. **Identify** Look at the list of materials that light passed through. What properties do these materials have in common?

____

____

Inquiry

Think of your own questions that you might test. What other materials would you like to test?

My Question Is:

____

How I Can Test It:

____

My Results Are:

____

Window Decorations

Materials

- construction materials as in Explore Activity
- tape
- string

Procedures

1. With a partner, plan how you will construct a "stained-glass" decoration to hang in a window. Your decoration must include at least four different materials that allow different amounts of light to pass through them. Be creative in your design. Draw or describe your design on a separate sheet of paper.
2. Use tape to construct your decoration.
3. Use string to hang your decoration in a window.

Conclude and Apply

Explain your choice of materials for your window decoration.

____

____

____

____

Light

In this topic you will learn about how light travels and how it affects matter.

Light is a form of energy. Sources of light include the Sun, the stars, light bulbs, and candles. Light travels in straight lines from its source. Light passes through some materials but not through others. For example, light passes through a glass window but not through a brick wall. A brick is opaque. **Opaque** materials do not allow any light to pass through them. Light rays that do not pass through a material reflect off it. **Reflect** means to bounce off a surface. When light rays reflect off a surface, they change the direction they are traveling in. You see objects because light reflected from the object enters your eyes. A mirror is very smooth and shiny. Light rays are reflected from a mirror. When you stand in front of a mirror, you see a face just like yours. This is your reflection. Light rays that are reflected from surfaces that are dull or rough are reflected in many different directions. You don't see a reflection when light is reflected in many different directions.

Light rays can change direction when they move from one material to another. For example, when light rays pass from air to water or from water to air, they bend. A spoon in a glass of water looks bent because the light rays are bent.

Light can change matter. A camera uses light to make photographs. The film inside the camera is coated with chemicals that change when light shines on them. Powerful beams of light, called lasers, can be strong enough to cut steel. Lasers are also used to read special codes of information on items at the supermarket.

Light

Fill in the blanks.

What Does Light Pass Through?

1. Light is a form of ________________.

2. Light can make ________________ move or change.

3. The Sun, lightning, and fire are all examples of ________________ sources of light.

4. Light travels in ________________________ from its source.

5. Materials that do not allow any light to pass through them are called ________________ materials.

6. Opaque materials create ________________.

7. Light rays that do not pass through a material ________________ ________________ from it.

8. Light rays change the ________________ in which they are traveling when they are reflected from a surface.

9. You see an object because light that is reflected from the object enters your ________________.

10. Light rays are reflected in many different directions from a rough ________________.

11. Light rays change direction when they move from one ________________ to another.

12. As light rays move from air to water or from water to air, they ________________.

Fill in the blanks.

Light Can Change Matter

13. A camera uses ________________ to make a photograph.

14. The film inside a camera is coated with ________________ that change when light shines on them.

15. Powerful beams of light that can cut steel are called ________________.

16. Lasers can read special codes of ________________ on items at the supermarket.

17. Plants cannot live and grow without ________________.

Light

The drawing shows what happens when light rays move from one material to another. Use the drawing to answer the following questions.

The spoon looks bent because the light rays bend as they pass from one material to another.

1. What solids are shown in the drawing?

____

2. What liquid is shown in the drawing?

____

3. List, in order, the kinds of matter that the light rays move through along their path.

____

____

4. Describe how the spoon looks.

____

____

5. Do you think the spoon really has this form? Explain your answer.

____

____

____

Using Variables

Controlling an Experiment

Variables are things in an experiment that can be changed or controlled. For example, suppose you wanted to answer the question: *What affects how light bends in a liquid?* Here are some variables that could be changed:

- the kind of liquid you use
- the size of the container you use
- the position of the object in the liquid

Procedures

1. **Compare** Take a close look at the containers in the picture. What differences do you see? Describe them below. These differences are variables. List all the variables you can identify on the left side of the table on the next page. The first variable is given.

____

____

____

____

2. Communicate Complete the table. After you identify as many variables as you can, indicate how you could control each variable.

____

____

____

____

Variable	Control
Container	

Conclude and Apply

Identify Which one variable would you change to see its effect on the bending of light? Why?

____

____

____

____

Name ____ CLOZE TEST 5

Light

Fill in the blanks.

Light is a form of ________________. There are many different sources of light. The Sun, stars, lightning, fire, and some living things are examples of sources of ________________ light. Light travels in ________________ lines from its source. Light passes through some materials but not through others. Materials that don't allow light to pass through them are ________________. Materials that block light create ________________.

Light

Which of these items are opaque and which are NOT opaque? Write each item in the correct list.

wood	plastic bottle	plastic wrap	cardboard
tin can	milk carton	plexiglass	brick
water	air		

OPAQUE	NOT OPAQUE
1.	**6.**
2.	**7.**
3.	**8.**
4.	**9.**
5.	**10.**

Answer these questions in your own words.

11. You are on a camping trip, and you have lost your mirror. What other surfaces could you use to see your reflection? What do these surfaces have in common?

____

____

____

12. Is light a form of energy? What are natural sources of light? What kind of light is made by people?

____

____

____

____

Investigate What Makes It Light

Hypothesize You often have to put parts together in a certain way for something to work. How can you put a light bulb, wire, and battery together so that the bulb lights? How might you test your ideas?

Write a **Hypothesis:**

____

____

Test what makes the bulb light by putting the parts together in different ways.

Materials

- D cell
- small light bulb
- 20 cm wire

Procedures

1. **Observe** Look at the bulb, wire, and cell. How do you think you might put these three things together to make the bulb light? Record any ideas you may have.

   ____

   ____

2. **Experiment** Try to light the bulb. Draw a picture of each set-up that you try on a separate sheet of paper. Record which ones work and which ones don't.

Conclude and Apply

1. **Identify** How many ways did you find to light the bulb? How many ways did you find that did not light the bulb?

   ____

2. **Compare and Contrast** How were the ways that worked to light the bulb alike? How were they different from the ways that did not work?

____

____

____

____

Going Further: Apply

3. **Draw Conclusions** How must the bulb, wire, and cell be put together so that the bulb will light?

____

____

____

Inquiry

Think of your own questions that you might test. Can you change your setup and still light the bulb?

My Question Is:

____

How I Can Test It:

____

My Results Are:

____

Time's Up!

Materials

- D cell battery
- small electric buzzer
- 20 cm wire

Procedures

1. Look at the buzzer, wire, and cell. How do you think you might put these three things together to make the buzzer buzz? Record your ideas.

   ____

   ____

   ____

2. Try to make the buzzer buzz. Draw each set-up that you try on a separate sheet of paper. Record which ones work and which ones don't.

   ____

   ____

   ____

Conclude and Apply

1. How many ways did you find to sound the buzzer? How many ways did you find that did not sound the buzzer?

   ____

   ____

2. How must the buzzer, wire, and cell be put together so that the buzzer will buzz?

   ____

   ____

   ____

Electricity

In this topic you will learn about some of the sources of electricity and the path electricity follows.

If a bulb, wire, and cell are put together in the correct way, the bulb will light. A **cell** is a source of electricity. These parts form a system. A system is a group of things that work together. The bulb, wire, and cell work as an electrical system. The system uses electric energy to light the bulb. Electricity is a form of energy that travels in a circuit. A **circuit** is the path electricity flows through. A circuit is like a train track. Just as the track must be complete before a train can travel on it, a circuit must be complete for electricity to flow. A complete circuit is called closed circuit. A closed circuit has no gaps. An open circuit has a gap. Electricity cannot flow through an open circuit.

You can control the flow of electricity. When you want to turn on a flashlight, you use a switch. A **switch** opens or closes an electric circuit. Pushing the switch one way closes the circuit. It allows electricity to flow in a complete path. The bulb lights up.

You use electricity at home. Almost everyone uses electric lights. You may also use electricity to heat your home. Electric machines include refrigerators, hair dryers, and vacuum cleaners. Radios, computers, and television sets all run on electricity.

In a toaster, electricity changes to heat as it flows through a wire. Electricity flows through an electric motor in a fan, causing the fan's blades to turn. Electricity makes a thin wire in a light bulb so hot that it glows.

Electricity

Fill in the blanks.

What Makes It Light?

1. A cell is a source of ______________.

2. A group of things that work together is called a(n) ______________.

3. A bulb, wire, and cell work together as a(n) ______________ system.

4. Electricity is a form of ______________ that travels in a circuit.

5. The path that electricity flows through is called a(n) ______________.

6. A circuit is like a train ______________.

7. A train needs a complete ______________ to travel on.

8. Electricity will flow through a complete path, which is called a(n) ______________.

9. A closed circuit has no ______________.

10. Electricity cannot flow through a(n) ______________ circuit.

How Can You Control the Flow of Electricity?

11. A(n) ______________ is used to open or close an electric circuit.

12. Pushing a switch one way allows electricity to ______________ in a complete path.

Fill in the blanks.

How Do You Use Electricity?

13. Many homes use ________________ lights.

14. Many people use ________________ to heat their homes.

15. Refrigerators, vacuum cleaners, and hair dryers are all electric ________________.

16. Radios and computers both run on ________________.

17. As electricity flows through a wire inside a toaster, it changes to ________________.

18. Electricity makes a thin wire inside a light bulb so hot that it ________________.

19. Electricity flows through an electric ________________ inside a fan, which causes the blades to spin.

Name ____________________ STUDY AID 6

Electricity

A chart is a way to organize information. This chart compares open circuits and closed circuits. The left column in the chart compares a circuit to a train track. The right column in the chart describes how electricity flows through a circuit.

Open and Closed Circuits

Ⓐ A circuit is like a train track. There must be a complete path for the train to travel. 	Electricity needs a closed circuit, or complete path, to flow. A closed circuit has no gaps. 
Ⓑ If there is a gap in the path, the train won't go. 	An open circuit has a gap. Electricity cannot flow through an open circuit. 

Use the chart to answer the following questions.

1. How is a circuit like a train track?

____

2. What will make a train stop moving along a track?

____

3. What will stop the flow of electricity?

____

Make a Flashlight

Hypothesize A flashlight is a source of light that uses cells as its source of electricity. How can you put the materials together to make a model of a flashlight?

Write a **Hypothesis:**

____

____

____

____

____

Materials

- 2 D cells
- paper tube
- 30 cm wire
- flashlight bulb

Procedures

Make a Model Use the materials provided for you to construct a model of a flashlight.

Conclude and Apply

1. **Explain** How is your model like a real flashlight? How is your model different?

____

____

____

____

____

____

2. **Communicate** Draw a diagram of your model flashlight's circuit on a separate sheet of paper. How are you able to turn your circuit on and off?

____

____

____

Going Further Electricity can flow through some types of materials but not others. How can you use a circuit to find out whether electricity can flow through certain materials? Write and conduct an experiment.

My Hypothesis Is:

____

____

My Experiment Is:

____

____

____

____

____

My Results Are:

____

____

____

Name ____ CLOZE TEST 6

Electricity

Fill in the blanks.

You can put together a cell, bulb, and wire to form a(n) ________________, or group of things that work together. Just like a train set, these parts have to be put together in a certain way for the system to work. These parts form an electrical ________________. Electricity is a form of ________________. The source of electricity is the ________________. The system uses electrical energy to light the ________________.

Electricity

Write these words to complete sentences 1–6.

open switch heat circuit closed cell

1. A path that electricity flows through is called a(n) ________________.

2. Electricity changes to ________________ when it flows through a toaster.

3. Electricity will not flow through a circuit that is ________________.

4. A device that is used to open or close an electrical circuit is called a(n) ________________.

5. You can play your CD player when its electrical circuit is ________________.

6. One source of electricity is called a(n) ________________.

Answer these questions in your own words.

7. Describe the closed circuit in a flashlight. Is the flashlight on or off when the circuit is closed?

____

____

____

8. A storm has caused the electricity in your home to go off. Which items that usually use electricity might still work? Why?

____

____

____

____

Energy

Circle the letter of the best answer.

1. Temperature is a measure of

a. cooked food. **b.** how cold it is.

c. how hot or cold something is. **d.** degrees.

2. Heat travels easily through a conductor, but does NOT travel easily through a(n)

a. insulator. **b.** thermometer.

c. solid. **d.** liquid.

3. Heat always flows from warmer objects to

a. the ground. **b.** hot objects.

c. plants. **d.** cooler objects.

4. Opaque items, which light cannot pass through, create

a. darkness. **b.** shadows.

c. energy. **d.** matter.

5. Light that does NOT pass through an object

a. looks white to the human eye. **b.** bends.

c. creates energy. **d.** is reflected off the object.

6. A cell is

a. a source of electricity.

b. a kind of circuit.

c. a form of energy.

d. something that opens and closes a circuit.

Circle the letter of the best answer.

7. When light rays pass from one material to another, they

a. disappear. **b.** break.

c. bend. **d.** make shadows.

8. The path that electricity follows is called a

a. cell. **b.** circuit.

c. switch. **d.** light.

9. When matter is heated, it

a. expands. **b.** changes form.

c. changes color. **d.** gets smaller.

10. Which of these items is NOT opaque?

a. a computer disk **b.** a window

c. a cell **d.** a movie screen

11. Heat is

a. a measure of temperature. **b.** a mixture.

c. a form of electricity. **d.** a form of energy.

12. A closed circuit

a. prevents electricity from flowing.

b. means you have a dead light bulb.

c. allows electricity to flow.

d. makes the temperature rise.

Name ______________________ EXPLORE ACTIVITY 1
Page 1

Investigate Which Object Takes Up More Space

Hypothesize What will happen when you put different objects in a container of water? How might you test your ideas?

Write a **Hypothesis:**

Possible hypothesis: The water level will rise when objects are added.

Test which object takes up more space by placing different objects in a container of water.

Materials

- 12-oz. plastic cup half full of water
- markers (different colors)
- a piece of clay
- classroom objects

Procedures

1. **Measure** Find the level of the water. Use a marker to mark the level on the outside of the cup. Children should find the water by viewing the cup at eye level.
2. **Predict** What will happen to the level of the water when you place the piece of clay in the cup? Record your prediction.
   Students will likely predict that the water level will rise.
3. **Observe** Place the clay in the cup. What happens? Use a different color marker to mark the new water level on the outside of the cup. Remove the clay.
   The water level goes up.
4. **Predict** Look at the other objects. Which object will make the water level change the most when you put it in the cup? Record your prediction.
   Students will likely predict that the largest object will cause the water to rise the most.
5. **Experiment** Place one object at a time in the cup. Mark the new water level for each object. Use a different color marker for each object.

Name ______________________ EXPLORE ACTIVITY 1
Investigate Which Object Takes Up More Space Page 2

Conclude and Apply

1. **Identify** What happened each time you placed an object in the cup? Why?
   The water level rose. The water and the object cannot be in the same space, so the water level went up.
2. **Compare and Contrast** How did the different objects affect the water level? Why do you think this happened?
   Large objects made the water level rise higher because they take up more space than small objects.
3. **Draw Conclusions** Which object takes up the most space? How do you know?
   The largest object takes up the most space. It caused the greatest change in the water level.

Going Further: Problem Solving

4. **Experiment** What do you think will happen to the water level in the cup if you change the shape of the clay?
   Nothing, because the clay will take up the same amount of space no matter what its shape.

Inquiry

Think of your own questions that you might like to test. Will a heavy object or a light object cause a greater change in the water level? Write your question, a way to test your question, and your results on a separate sheet of paper.

Possible question: Do two objects that are about the same size but different weights cause the water level to rise the same amount?
Possible test: Repeat the experiment using a coin and a plastic counter that are about the same size. Results: The change in water level is the same. As long as the objects take up the same amount of space, their weight does not affect the change in water level.

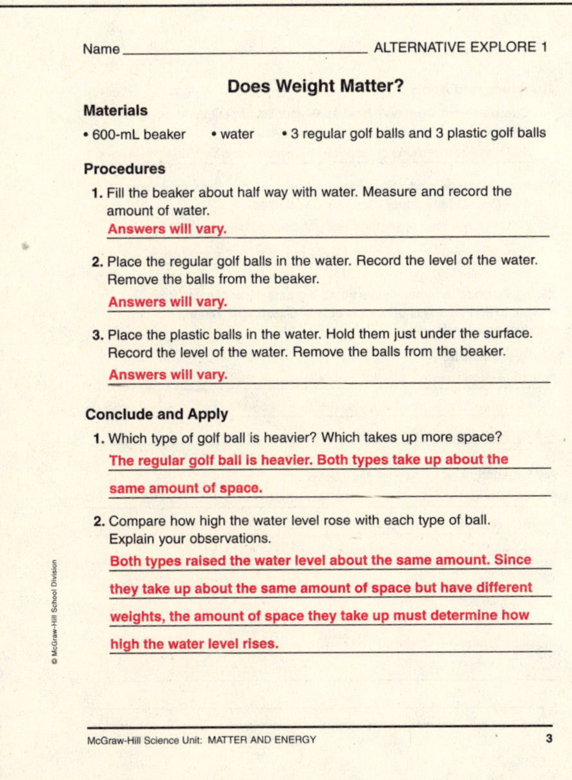

Name ______________________ ALTERNATIVE EXPLORE 1

Does Weight Matter?

Materials

- 600-mL beaker
- water
- 3 regular golf balls and 3 plastic golf balls

Procedures

1. Fill the beaker about half way with water. Measure and record the amount of water.
   Answers will vary.
2. Place the regular golf balls in the water. Record the level of the water. Remove the balls from the beaker.
   Answers will vary.
3. Place the plastic balls in the water. Hold them just under the surface. Record the level of the water. Remove the balls from the beaker.
   Answers will vary.

Conclude and Apply

1. Which type of golf ball is heavier? Which takes up more space?
   The regular golf ball is heavier. Both types take up about the same amount of space.
2. Compare how high the water level rose with each type of ball. Explain your observations.
   Both types raised the water level about the same amount. Since they take up about the same amount of space but have different weights, the amount of space they take up must determine how high the water level rises.

Name ______________________ READING STUDY GUIDE 1
Page 1

Rocks, Clocks, Trees, and Bees

Fill in the blanks.

Which Object Takes Up More Space?

1. Since a brick and a pencil both take up space, they are both types of **matter**.
2. The more space an object takes up, the greater its **volume**.
3. Since a tennis ball takes up less space than a soccer ball, a tennis ball has less **volume** than a soccer ball.
4. The amount of matter that is in an object is called its **mass**.
5. The mass of an apple is **less** than the mass of a school bus.
6. Since the particles in a book are packed more tightly than the particles in a balloon, a book has more **mass** than a balloon.

How Do You Measure Mass?

7. The unit that is used to measure mass is a **gram**.
8. Since a school bus is large, its mass is measured in **kilograms**.
9. Since a paper clip is small, its mass is measured in **grams**.
10. One kilogram is equal to **1,000** grams.

Name ______________________ READING STUDY GUIDE 1
Rocks, Clocks, Trees, and Bees Page 2

Fill in the blanks.

How Else Can You Describe Matter?

11. A property is a(n) **characteristic** of an object.
12. Two properties of all matter are volume and **mass**.
13. Size and shape are two **properties** of matter.
14. A property of a raft is that it **floats** in water.

How Are Mass and Weight Related?

15. The greater the mass of an object, the greater its **weight**.
16. The weight of an object is the pull of **gravity** on that object.
17. As the mass of two objects increases, the pull of gravity between the objects **increases**.
18. As the distance between two objects increases, the pull of gravity between the objects **decreases**.
19. Since the Moon has less **mass** than Earth, the pull of gravity is weaker on the Moon than on Earth.

Name ______________________ QUICK LAB 1
Page 1

Measuring Mass

Hypothesize Do objects in your classroom have different masses?

Write a **Hypothesis:**

Possible hypothesis: Objects in the classroom have different masses.

Materials

- balance
- small objects
- 30 paper clips

Procedures

1. Estimate the mass of each object. Record your estimates.
   Possible answer: Estimates depend on the objects selected and the student's reasoning.
2. **Measure** Measure the mass of each object. Place the object on one side of the balance. Place paper clips on the other side until the two sides balance. Record the number of paper clips used to balance each object in the table below.
3. **Use Numbers** What is the mass of each object? (Remember, two paper clips equals about one gram.) Record the mass of each object in the table.

Object	Number of Paper Clips	Mass of Object
	Mass in grams = (number of paper clips) divided by (2 paper clips per gram)	

Name ______________________ QUICK LAB 1
Measuring Mass Page 2

Conclude and Apply

1. **Compare and Contrast** How does your list of estimated masses compare with the measurements you recorded?
   The answers depend on student estimates and the objects tested.
2. **Plan** If you wanted to find the mass of your shoe, how could you do it? How many paper clips would you need?
   Find the number of paper clips needed to balance the shoe. A 500-gram shoe (about 1 lb) would require 1000 paper clips.

Going Further A nickel equals about 5 grams. How can you use nickels to find the mass of objects in your classroom? Write and conduct an experiment.

My Hypothesis Is:

Possible hypothesis: You can use nickels to find the mass of objects by placing nickels on a balance until the two sides balance and then multiplying the number of nickels by 5.

My Experiment Is:

Possible experiment: Place an object on one side of the balance. Place nickels on the other side until the two sides balance. Record the number of nickels and multiply by 5.

My Results Are:

mass in grams = (number of nickels) multiplied by (5 grams per nickel)

Name ______________________ STUDY AID 1

Rocks, Clocks, Trees, and Bees

A diagram uses pictures and words to describe a thing or a process. This diagram shows a boy and a cat on Earth, on the Moon, and on Jupiter. The labels tell you that the diagram has information about the weight and mass of the boy and the cat. Use the diagram to answer the following questions.

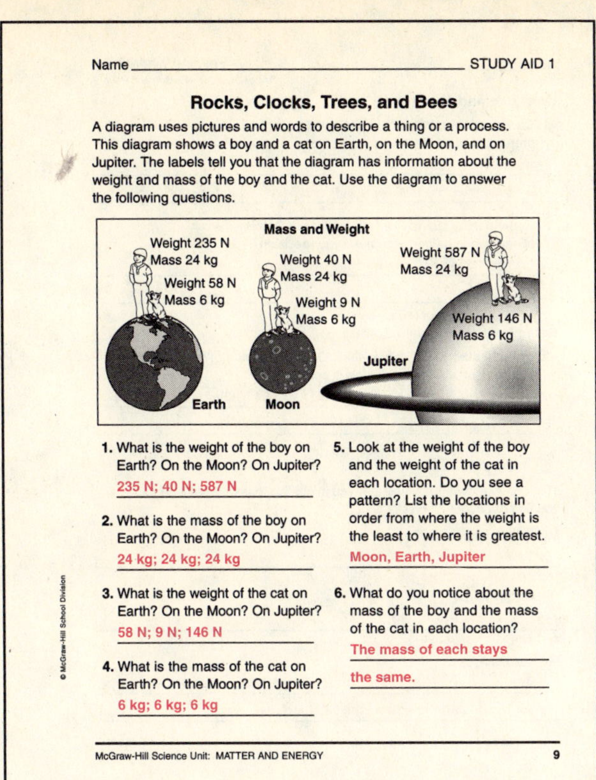

1. What is the weight of the boy on Earth? On the Moon? On Jupiter? 235 N; 40 N; 587 N
2. What is the mass of the boy on Earth? On the Moon? On Jupiter? 24 kg; 24 kg; 24 kg
3. What is the weight of the cat on Earth? On the Moon? On Jupiter? 58 N; 9 N; 146 N
4. What is the mass of the cat on Earth? On the Moon? On Jupiter? 6 kg; 6 kg; 6 kg
5. Look at the weight of the boy and the weight of the cat in each location. Do you see a pattern? List the locations in order from where the weight is the least to where it is greatest. Moon, Earth, Jupiter
6. What do you notice about the mass of the boy and the mass of the cat in each location? The mass of each stays the same.

Name ______________________ CLOZE TEST 1

Rocks, Clocks, Trees, and Bees

Fill in the blanks.

You can describe an object by naming a(n) property, or characteristic, of the object. All matter has volume and mass. Other properties are special for each type of matter, for example, size, shape, color, and texture. There are more properties you can use to describe matter. For example, some objects float in water and other objects sink.

Name ______________________ TOPIC PRACTICE 1

Rocks, Clocks, Trees, and Bees

Use one of these words to complete sentences 1–6.

gravity	space	properties
matter	particles	volume

1. The amount of space an object takes up is called its volume.
2. Mass is a measure of how much matter an object contains.
3. The weight of an object is the pull of gravity on the object.
4. All matter is made up of particles.
5. Matter is anything that takes up space and has mass.
6. You can describe matter by naming its properties.

Answer these questions in your own words.

7. You have one bag of trash with a mass of 3 kg and another bag of trash with a mass of 14 kg. What do you know about the weights of the bags of trash? The bag with the greater mass also has the greater weight.
8. You have a bowl of pancake batter. You add a quart of blueberries to the batter. What happens to the level of the batter in the bowl when you add the blueberries? The level of the batter in the bowl will rise.
9. A dog weighs 70 N on Earth. If the dog is sent to the Moon, how would its weight change? How would its mass change? The dog would weigh less on the Moon. Its mass would remain the same.

Name ______________________ EXPLORE ACTIVITY 2
Page 1

Design Your Own Experiment

How Can You Classify Matter?

Hypothesize How can you tell whether a material is a solid or a liquid? How might you test your ideas?

Write a **Hypothesis:**

Possible hypothesis: You can tell if matter is a liquid or solid by observing its properties. Solids have a definite shape and volume, while liquids have a definite volume, but change shape freely.

Materials

- investigation tools
- plastic container of Oobleck
- newspaper
- safety goggles

Procedures **Safety** Wear goggles.

1. **Observe** Observe the Oobleck using only your senses. How does the Oobleck look? What does it feel like? Record all of your observations.
   Possible answer: Oobleck looks green and it feels soft and wet.
2. **Experiment** Using the tools given to you, investigate the Oobleck in different ways. What new things do you observe? Record these observations.
   When a force is slowly applied to Oobleck it changes shape, but Oobleck resists changing shape when force is quickly applied.
3. **Classify** Look at the observations of Oobleck that you have made. Then review the definitions of solid and liquid that you wrote. Do you think Oobleck is a solid or a liquid? Could it be both? Why?
   Answers may vary. Accept all answers with logical reasoning, for example: Oobleck is a liquid because it can change shape.

Name ______________________ EXPLORE ACTIVITY 2
Design Your Own Experiment Page 2

Conclude and Apply

1. **Communicate** What observations did you make about the properties of Oobleck? Children should describe the shape, smell, color, and texture of the substance. The shape is variable, the color is green, and the texture is soft and pasty. It should not have a strong smell.
2. **Explain** How did you decide to classify Oobleck? What observations helped you make your decision?
   Explanations should refer to the properties of shape and volume. (Oobleck actually has the properties of both a solid and liquid.)

Going Further: Problem Solving

3. **Hypothesize** What do you think Oobleck is made of? How might you find out whether your idea is correct?
   Children might suggest flour, water, or salt. They might combine different materials to try to duplicate Oobleck.

Inquiry

Think of your own questions that you might like to test. What else can you find out about Oobleck?

My Question Is:
Possible question: Is Oobleck a mixture of water and another substance?

How I Can Test It:
Possible test: Leave some Oobleck in an open container and see if it hardens.

My Results Are:
Possible answer: If Oobleck is left in an open container, the water will evaporate and the substance will harden.

Name ______________________ ALTERNATIVE EXPLORE 2

Changing Forms

Materials

- ice cubes
- cups of water

Procedures

1. Observe the ice and water. Record their properties.
   Possible properties: ice: cold, hard; water: warm, wet
2. Decide what type of matter the ice and water are, and explain your decision.
   Students might indicate that the ice is a solid because it is hard and the water is a liquid because it takes the shape of its container.
3. Think of a way that you could change the ice into water. Write your plan on a separate sheet of paper. Show your plan to your teacher. Once your teacher has approved your plan, try it. Observe and record your results.
   Answers will vary.

Conclude and Apply

1. How did the properties of the ice change when you tried your plan?
   The ice changed from a hard, cold solid that held its shape to a warmer, wet liquid that flowed.
2. How can you tell when something is a solid? A liquid?
   Accept all reasonable responses.

Name ______________________ READING STUDY GUIDE 2
Page 1

Comparing Solids, Liquids, and Gases

Fill in the blanks.

How Can You Classify Matter?

1. Solids, liquids, and gases are alike in that they all take up space and have ___mass___.
2. All solids have a definite shape and ___volume___.
3. All liquids have a(n) ___definite___ volume.
4. A liquid does not have a definite ___shape___.
5. Since milk takes the shape of the container it is in, it is a(n) ___liquid___.
6. A gas has no definite shape or ___volume___.
7. Both a gas and a(n) ___liquid___ take the shape of the container they are in.
8. All solids, liquids, and gases are made of ___particles___.
9. The particles in a solid form a certain ___pattern___.
10. The particles in a liquid have more ___energy___ than the particles in a solid.
11. The particles in a gas have more energy than the particles in a solid or a ___liquid___.
12. The particles in a(n) ___gas___ can spread out to fill a large container or squeeze together to fit a small container.

McGraw-Hill Science Unit: MATTER AND ENERGY 17

Name ______________________ READING STUDY GUIDE 2
Comparing Solids, Liquids, and Gases Page 2

Fill in the blanks.

How Can Matter Change?

13. Matter can change form and still be the same type of ___matter___.
14. Ice becomes liquid water when it ___melts___.
15. Water that evaporates changes from a liquid to a(n) ___gas___.
16. Particles in water vapor have more ___energy___ than the particles in solid or liquid water.

Can You Mix Different Kinds of Matter Together?

17. A mixture is a combination of different forms of ___matter___.
18. The properties of each type of matter in a(n) ___mixture___ do not change.

What Is a Different Kind of Mixture?

19. When one or more types of matter are spread evenly throughout another type of matter, a ___solution___ is formed.
20. Salt water is a type of ___solution___.

18 McGraw-Hill Science Unit: MATTER AND ENERGY

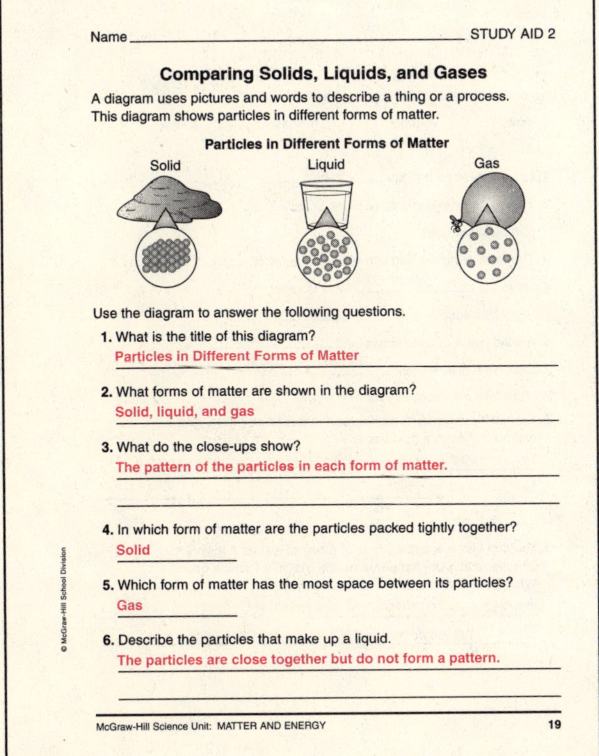

Name ______________________ STUDY AID 2

Comparing Solids, Liquids, and Gases

A diagram uses pictures and words to describe a thing or a process. This diagram shows particles in different forms of matter.

Particles in Different Forms of Matter

Use the diagram to answer the following questions.

1. What is the title of this diagram?
   Particles in Different Forms of Matter
2. What forms of matter are shown in the diagram?
   Solid, liquid, and gas
3. What do the close-ups show?
   The pattern of the particles in each form of matter.
4. In which form of matter are the particles packed tightly together?
   Solid
5. Which form of matter has the most space between its particles?
   Gas
6. Describe the particles that make up a liquid.
   The particles are close together but do not form a pattern.

McGraw-Hill Science Unit: MATTER AND ENERGY 19

Name ______________________ SKILL BUILDER 2
Page 1

Communicating

Making a Table

When you communicate you share information with others. Scientists communicate what they learn from an experiment. They might tell people how they think new information can be used. You can communicate by talking, or by creating a drawing, chart, table, or graph.

You can communicate what you know about the properties of solids, liquids, and gases. Look at the drawing on this page to help you answer the questions below.

Procedures

1. **Observe** Look at the drawing. What forms of matter do you see? What properties do these forms have? Record your observations.
Possible answer: Ice is a solid with a definite shape and a definite volume. Water is a liquid with a definite volume, but no definite shape. Air is a gas with no definite volume or definite shape.

Name ______________________ SKILL BUILDER 2
Communicating Page 2

2. **Communicate** Use your observations to fill in the table.

Forms of Matter	Properties
solid (ice)	Definite shape and definite volume
liquid (water)	Definite volume, but no definite shape
gas (air)	No definite volume or definite shape

Conclude and Apply

1. **Draw Conclusions** What do solids and liquids have in common? What makes them different?
Possible answer: Neither solids nor liquids change their volume. Liquids change their shape freely, but solids do not.

2. **Communicate** Give an example of a solid, a liquid, and a gas. Then write a sentence that tells what you know about the shape and volume of each one.
Students should explain that their example of a solid does not change shape or volume, their example of a liquid changes shape but not volume, and their example of a gas changes shape and volume.

Name ______________________ CLOZE TEST 2

Comparing Solids, Liquids, and Gases

Fill in the blanks.

When water changes to a solid form, it is called ice. As ice melts, it changes from a solid into a(n) liquid. The particles in water have more energy than the particles in ice. If water is warmed, it evaporates and changes into a gas. This gas is called water vapor. The particles in water vapor have more energy than the particles in water.

Name ______________________ TOPIC PRACTICE 2

Comparing Solids, Liquids, and Gases

Use one of these words to complete sentences 1–7.

solid	volume	mixture	shape
gas	solution	energy	

1. Liquids have no definite shape.
2. The particles in a gas have more energy than the particles in a solid.
3. The form of matter that can change volume is gas.
4. Ice is the solid form of water.
5. Vegetable soup is a(n) mixture.
6. A solid has a definite shape and volume.
7. Chocolate milk is a(n) solution.

Answer these questions in your own words.

8. Can all three forms of matter exist in a mixture? If so, give an example of such a mixture.
Yes, all three forms can exist in a mixture. An example would be a fish tank, soil, or a human body.

9. You can shape a certain type of material just as if it were clay. Left alone at room temperature, the material forms a puddle. What form of matter is the material? Why?
Answers may vary. Accept all responses with logical reasoning, for example: the material is a liquid, because it does not have a definite shape.

Name ____________________ EXPLORE ACTIVITY 3
Page 1

Investigate What Magnets Attract

Hypothesize What kinds of items will be attracted to a magnet?

Write a **Hypothesis:**

Possible hypothesis: The objects with metal parts will be attracted to the magnet.

Materials

- magnet
- several objects

Procedures

1. **Observe** Look at your objects. What properties of the objects do you observe? Record your observations.
   The properties will vary depending on the objects selected.
2. **Predict** Which of the objects will be attracted to a magnet? Record your predictions. The children might predict that metal objects or objects made from iron and steel will be attracted to the magnet.
3. **Experiment** Test your predictions. Get a magnet from your teacher. Test each object to see if it is attracted to the magnet. Record the result of each test.
   The answers depend upon the objects selected for testing. Most of the objects that contain metal will be attracted to the magnet.

Conclude and Apply

1. **Classify** Look at the results of your tests. Which objects were attracted to the magnet? Which objects were not? Make two lists on a separate sheet of paper. In one list, write the names of the objects attracted to the magnet. In the other list, write those that were not. Title each of the lists. Items listed as being attracted to the magnet should contain metals. Most objects listed as not being attracted to the magnet should not contain metals.

Name ____________________ EXPLORE ACTIVITY 3
Investigate What Magnets Attract Page 2

2. **Compare and Contrast** Read the list of objects that were attracted to the magnet. Can you identify any properties that they all have in common? Write down your thoughts. Now look at the list of objects that were not attracted to the magnet. What kinds of things can you say about these objects? Write down your thoughts.
   Attracted objects contain some metal. Some objects with metal parts and non-metallic objects were not attracted to the magnet.

Going Further: Apply

3. What conclusions can you draw about the kinds of things that are attracted to magnets?
   Objects attracted to magnets contain some metal, but not all metallic objects are attracted to magnets. Non-metallic objects are not attracted to magnets.

Inquiry

Think of your own questions that you might like to test. Can a magnet be used to separate objects?

My Question Is:

Possible question: Can a magnet attract paper clips in a pile of beads?

How I Can Test It:

Possible test: Test by placing beads in a pile with paper clips and moving a magnet over the mixture.

My Results Are:

Possible answer: The magnet attracted all of the paper clips.

Name ____________________ ALTERNATIVE EXPLORE 3

Treasure Hunt

Materials

- small objects
- large, deep pan of sand
- magnet

Procedures

1. Observe the objects. Predict whether or not you will be able to find each object using a magnet when the objects are buried in sand. Record your predictions.
   Predictions will vary, but the items made of metal should be considered magnetic while all other objects should not be considered magnetic.
2. Bury the objects in the sand.
3. Using only the magnet, locate as many buried objects as you can. Record the objects that you find.
   Results will depend on objects.

Conclude and Apply

1. Which objects did you find with the magnet? Why were you able to find some objects with the magnet but not all?
   Students should be able to find objects made of iron or steel using the magnet. They should indicate that only objects attracted to the magnet could be found.
2. Compare the objects you found with the magnet. How are they alike?
   They are made wholly or partly of metal.

Name ______________________ READING STUDY GUIDE 3
Page 1

Building Blocks of Matter

Fill in the blanks.

What Do Magnets Attract?

1. Magnets attract items that are made of some types of **metal**.
2. A magnet will **attract** a metal spoon.
3. Objects that are made from iron and steel have the property of **magnetism**.
4. Magnetism is the property of an object that makes it attract **iron** and some other metals.
5. Junkyards use the property of magnetism to lift and sort objects made of **metal**.
6. Natural magnets come from a rock called **magnetite**.
7. Magnetite is not as strong as a(n) **permanent** magnet.

What Are Some Other Uses of Iron and Steel?

8. Iron is mixed with other materials to make metals with different **properties**.
9. Steel is a metal that is made from **iron**.
10. You get iron from meats and dark green **vegetables**.
11. You get iron from fortified **cereals**.

Name ______________________ READING STUDY GUIDE 3
Building Blocks of Matter Page 2

Fill in the blanks.

What Are Some Other Metals?

12. Gold, silver, aluminum, and copper are all types of **metals**.
13. Each metal has its own special **properties**.
14. **Steel** is a heavy, hard metal.
15. Copper and **aluminum** are two light, soft metals.
16. Iron and gold are both **elements**, or building blocks of matter.
17. An element can be a solid, liquid, or **gas**.
18. A(n) **atom** is the smallest particle of matter.

How Can You Put Elements Together?

19. Iron and oxygen form a(n) **compound** called rust.
20. The properties of a compound are different from the properties of the **elements** that make it up.

Name ______________________ QUICK LAB 3
Page 1

Bowl of Iron

Hypothesize If you read the label on a box of breakfast cereal, you'll probably see iron in the list of ingredients. Does breakfast cereal really contain iron?

Write a **Hypothesis:**
Possible hypothesis: Breakfast cereal contains tiny particles of iron.

Materials

- 1 package fortified cereal
- plastic sandwich bag
- magnet
- sheet of white paper

Procedures

1. Pour the cereal into a plastic bag. Add the magnet and seal the bag.
2. Shake the bag for several minutes. Carefully remove the magnet. Hold it over a sheet of white paper.
3. **Observe** What do you see when you look at the magnet?
Possible answer: There are tiny, dark particles on the magnet and white paper.

Conclude and Apply

Predict What would happen if you tried the same experiment using cereal that did not contain iron?
Possible answer: Dark particles would not appear on the magnet.

Name ______________________ QUICK LAB 3
Bowl of Iron Page 2

Going Further Do different breakfast cereals contain different amounts of iron? How can you compare the amount of iron in different cereals? Write and conduct an experiment.

My Hypothesis Is:
Possible Hypothesis: Different breakfast cereals contain different amounts of iron.

My Experiment Is:
Possible Experiment: Place an equal amount of a variety of breakfast cereals in plastic bags. Place a magnet in each bag and shake the bag. Remove the magnet and hold it over a sheet of white paper. Compare the number of dark particles on the magnet and paper.

My Results Are:
Answers will vary depending on cereals tested.

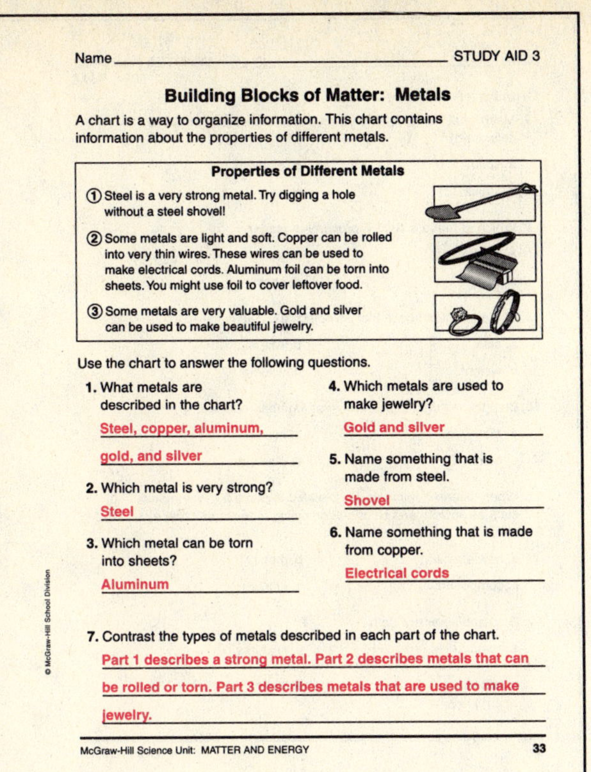

Name ______________________ STUDY AID 3

Building Blocks of Matter: Metals

A chart is a way to organize information. This chart contains information about the properties of different metals.

Properties of Different Metals

① Steel is a very strong metal. Try digging a hole without a steel shovel!

② Some metals are light and soft. Copper can be rolled into very thin wires. These wires can be used to make electrical cords. Aluminum foil can be torn into sheets. You might use foil to cover leftover food.

③ Some metals are very valuable. Gold and silver can be used to make beautiful jewelry.

Use the chart to answer the following questions.

1. What metals are described in the chart?
   Steel, copper, aluminum, gold, and silver
2. Which metal is very strong?
   Steel
3. Which metal can be torn into sheets?
   Aluminum
4. Which metals are used to make jewelry?
   Gold and silver
5. Name something that is made from steel.
   Shovel
6. Name something that is made from copper.
   Electrical cords
7. Contrast the types of metals described in each part of the chart.
   Part 1 describes a strong metal. Part 2 describes metals that can be rolled or torn. Part 3 describes metals that are used to make jewelry.

Name ______________________ STUDY AID 3

Building Blocks of Matter: Compounds

A chart is a way to organize information. This chart contains information about common compounds. Each row describes a different compound. The top line in each row names the elements and the compound that they form. The bottom line in each row names properties of the elements and the compound.

COMMON COMPOUNDS

Element		Element		Compound	
Sodium a soft metal	+	**Chlorine** a poisonous green gas	=	**Sodium Chloride** table salt, white not poisonous	
Hydrogen a gas that is lighter than air	+	**Oxygen** a gas	=	**Water** a liquid that is 1,000 times heavier than air	
Iron a hard metal	+	**Oxygen** a gas	=	**Rust** a soft, reddish crust	

Use the chart to answer the following questions.

1. What compound is described in the first row?
   Sodium chloride
2. What compound is described in the last row?
   Rust
3. What poisonous green gas is an element that forms sodium chloride?
   Chlorine
4. What two elements make water?
   Hydrogen and oxygen
5. What hard metal is an element that forms rust?
   Iron
6. What compound is used as table salt?
   Sodium chloride
7. Describe hydrogen.
   Hydrogen is a gas that is lighter than air.

Name ______________________ CLOZE TEST 3

Building Blocks of Matter

Fill in the blanks.

Magnets attract objects made of some types of __metal__. A metal is a shiny material that can be found in the __ground__. Many of the objects that magnets attract are made from the metals iron and __steel__. Objects made from iron and steel have the property of __magnetism__. The property of magnetism can be used to identify objects. Junkyards use powerful __magnets__ to lift and sort objects made of metal.

Name ______________________ TOPIC PRACTICE 3

Building Blocks of Matter

Use one of these words to complete sentences 1–8.

iron	matter	atoms	ground
elements	metal	aluminum	compound

1. If an object is attracted to a magnet, it must be made of __metal__.
2. Metals are found in the __ground__.
3. Steel is a metal that is made with __iron__.
4. Elements are the building blocks of __matter__.
5. All elements are made of __atoms__.
6. If the properties of elements change when they are mixed together, the mixture is called a(n) __compound__.
7. One metal that is light and soft is __aluminum__.
8. Your body contains about 11 different __elements__.

Answer these questions in your own words.

9. Which elements are found in water? How is the compound different from its elements?
   Hydrogen and oxygen are used to make water. The elements are both gases, but water is a liquid.
10. How can magnets be used for work?
    They can be used in a junkyard to sort metal objects.

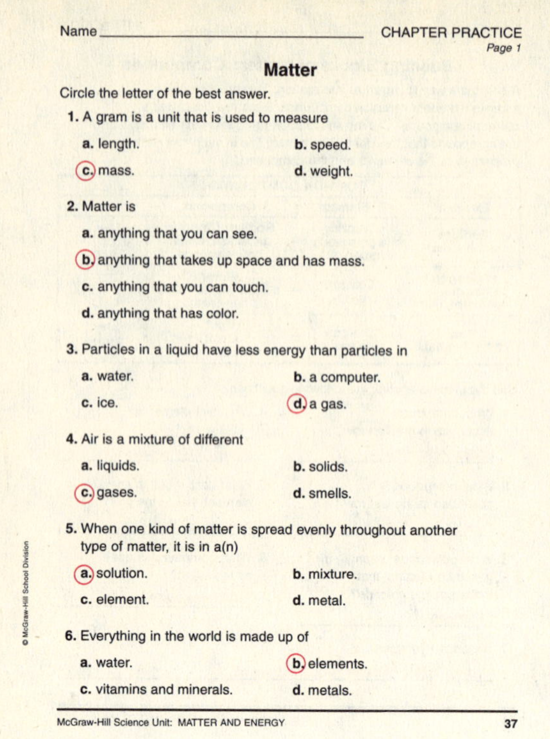

Name ______________________ CHAPTER PRACTICE
Page 1

Matter

Circle the letter of the best answer.

1. A gram is a unit that is used to measure
   a. length. b. speed.
   c. mass. d. weight.
2. Matter is
   a. anything that you can see.
   b. anything that takes up space and has mass.
   c. anything that you can touch.
   d. anything that has color.
3. Particles in a liquid have less energy than particles in
   a. water. b. a computer.
   c. ice. d. a gas.
4. Air is a mixture of different
   a. liquids. b. solids.
   c. gases. d. smells.
5. When one kind of matter is spread evenly throughout another type of matter, it is in a(n)
   a. solution. b. mixture.
   c. element. d. metal.
6. Everything in the world is made up of
   a. water. b. elements.
   c. vitamins and minerals. d. metals.

Name ______________________ CHAPTER PRACTICE
Matter Page 2

Circle the letter of the best answer.

7. Matter that has a definite volume but not a definite shape is called a(n)
   a. solid. b. element.
   c. liquid. d. gas.
8. Which of these is NOT a property of matter?
   a. an opinion b. size
   c. color d. shape
9. The amount of space that an object takes up is called its
   a. size. b. shape.
   c. weight. d. volume.
10. Blending different types of matter together makes a(n)
    a. metal. b. mixture.
    c. atom. d. element.
11. When different elements are blended to make a new material, such as sodium and chlorine combining to make salt, the result is called a
    a. new element. b. metal.
    c. compound. d. mixture.
12. Gold and silver are both
    a. compounds. b. mixtures.
    c. metals. d. liquids.

Name ______________________ EXPLORE ACTIVITY 4
Page 1

Investigate How Heat Affects Different Materials

Hypothesize You could measure how hot soil and water get when they are exposed to the same amount of heat. Would one type of matter warm up more than the other? How might you test your ideas?

Write a **Hypothesis:** Possible hypothesis: When different types of matter are exposed to the same amount of heat they do not warm up an equal amount.

Materials

- soil
- water
- 2 foam cups
- 2 thermometers
- heat source (sunlight or lamp)

Procedures

1. Fill one of the cups with water. Place an equal amount of soil in the other cup.
2. **Measure** Using your thermometers, measure how warm the soil and water are. Record your measurements.
   Answers will vary depending on room temperature.
3. Estimate how hot the soil and water will get if they are left in a warm place for 15 minutes. Record your estimates, then place the soil and water near a heat source. Make sure they are the same distance from the heat source.
   Answers will vary. The soil will get hotter than the water.
4. **Measure** Record the readings on the thermometers every 5 minutes for 15 minutes. Student findings will vary.
5. **Use Numbers** Find the difference between the first thermometer reading and the last. To do this, subtract the first measurement you made from the last measurement you made.
   Temperature changes for soil and water will vary.

Name ______________________ EXPLORE ACTIVITY 4
Investigate How Heat Affects Different Materials Page 2

Conclude and Apply

1. **Identify** Which type of matter warmed up more? How do you know?
   Possible answers: The soil warmed up more because the difference between the start and end temperature was greater. (Children may quote actual temperatures.)
2. **Compare and Contrast** Were your estimates close to your actual measurements?
   Answers will vary depending on student predictions.

Going Further: Apply

3. **Infer** Why is it important to place the soil and water an equal distance from the heat source?
   The soil and water are placed equal distances from the heat source so that they receive the same amount of heat.

Inquiry

Think of your own questions that you might test. Which would get hotter when they are exposed to the same amount of heat—sand or water?

My Question Is:
Possible question: Does sand heat up faster than water?

How I Can Test It:
Possible test: Prepare a cup of sand and a cup of water. Place both cups by a heat source and measure the temperature changes.

My Results Are:
Possible answer: Sand will heat up faster than water.

Name ______________________ ALTERNATIVE EXPLORE 4

Black and White

Materials

- black paper
- white paper
- two thermometers

Procedures

1. Cover one thermometer with black paper. Cover the other thermometer with white paper.
2. Place the thermometers in a sunny spot or under a lamp.
3. Predict which thermometer will have a higher reading after 5 minutes. Record your prediction.
   Predictions will vary.
4. Wait 5 minutes. Observe and record the thermometer readings.
   Results will vary.

Conclude and Apply

1. Which thermometer had a higher reading? Explain why.
   The thermometer covered with black paper had a higher reading because black absorbs heat better than white.
2. What colors would be more comfortable to wear in hot weather? In cold weather?
   light colors; dark colors

Name ______________________ READING STUDY GUIDE 4
Page 1

Heat

Fill in the blanks.

How Does Heat Affect Different Materials?

1. Heat affects different types of matter in different ways.
2. You can measure how much matter warms up by using a(n) thermometer.
3. Thermometers measure temperature, which is how hot or cold an object is.
4. The unit of measurement for temperature is the degree.
5. Energy makes matter move or change.
6. A form of energy that makes matter warmer is heat.
7. Heat can be added to an object to raise the object's temperature.
8. It takes more energy to heat water than to heat soil to the same temperature.
9. The diagram shows that heat always flows from warmer objects to cooler ones.
10. In the diagram, heat flowed from the warm air to the cold ice.
11. In the diagram, heat flowed from the hot liquid to the boy's cold hands.

Name ______________________ READING STUDY GUIDE 4
Heat Page 2

Fill in the blanks.

How Does Heat Change Matter?

12. Heat is a form of energy.
13. When a thermometer is in a warm place, the liquid inside it expands.
14. Heat causes the particles in matter to move faster.
15. When matter loses heat, its particles slow down.
16. As matter contracts, it takes up less space.

How Can You Control the Flow of Heat?

17. Heat moves quickly through many metals.
18. An insulator is a material that heat doesn't travel through easily.
19. Wool and cotton are both good insulators.

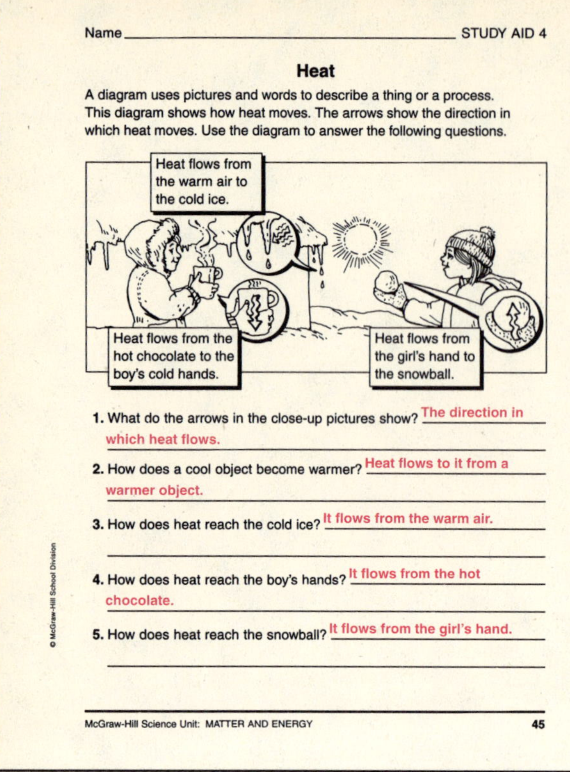

Name ______________________ STUDY AID 4

Heat

A diagram uses pictures and words to describe a thing or a process. This diagram shows how heat moves. The arrows show the direction in which heat moves. Use the diagram to answer the following questions.

1. What do the arrows in the close-up pictures show? The direction in which heat flows.
2. How does a cool object become warmer? Heat flows to it from a warmer object.
3. How does heat reach the cold ice? It flows from the warm air.
4. How does heat reach the boy's hands? It flows from the hot chocolate.
5. How does heat reach the snowball? It flows from the girl's hand.

Name ______________________ QUICK LAB 4
Page 1

Expand and Contract

Hypothesize Do gases expand when heated? Do they contract when cooled?

Write a **Hypothesis:**
Possible hypothesis: Gases expand when heated and contract when cooled.

Materials

- balloon
- 2L plastic bottle
- bucket of warm water
- bucket of cool water

Procedures

1. Stretch the opening of the balloon over the opening of the bottle.
2. **Predict** What will happen when you place the bottle in the bucket of warm water? Test your prediction.
   Possible answer: When the bottle is placed in warm water the balloon will get bigger because the air in the bottle will warm up and expand.
3. **Predict** What will happen when you place the bottle in the bucket of cool water? Test your prediction.
   Possible answer: When the bottle is placed in cool water the balloon will shrink because the air inside the bottle will cool and contract.

Name ______________________ QUICK LAB 4
Expand and Contract Page 2

Conclude and Apply

1. **Communicate** What happened to the balloon when you placed it in warm water? In cold water?
   Possible answer: When the bottle was placed in warm water the balloon got bigger. When the bottle was placed in cool water the balloon shrank.
2. **Draw Conclusions** What happened to the air particles in the balloon when the bottle was in the warm water? The cool water?
   Possible answer: The warm water heated the air particles causing them to move faster and farther apart from each other. The cool water cooled the air particles so they slowed down and moved closer together.

Going Further Does the size of the bottle affect how the balloon expands? Write and conduct an experiment.

My Hypothesis Is:
Possible hypothesis: Using a smaller bottle will make the balloon expand less than a larger bottle.

My Experiment Is:
Possible experiment: Conduct the same experiment with a smaller plastic bottle.

My Results Are:
Possible answer: The balloon expanded less when a smaller bottle was placed in a bucket of warm water.

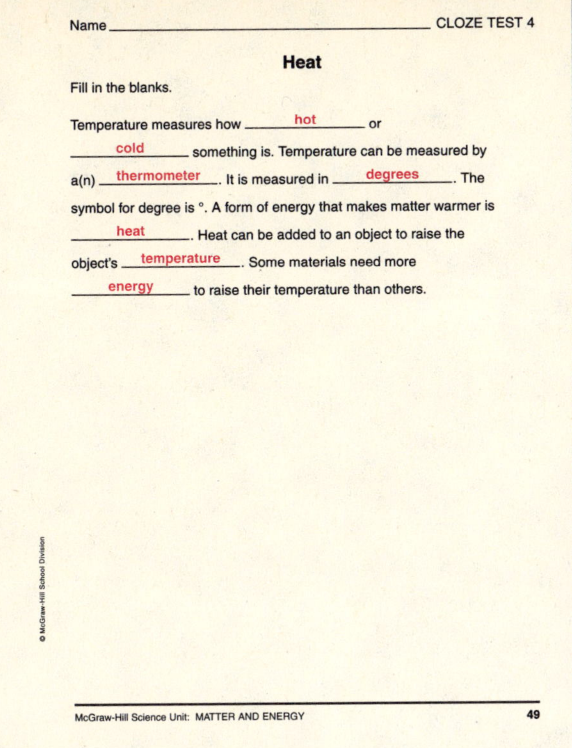

Name ______________________ CLOZE TEST 4

Heat

Fill in the blanks.

Temperature measures how ___hot___ or ___cold___ something is. Temperature can be measured by a(n) ___thermometer___. It is measured in ___degrees___. The symbol for degree is °. A form of energy that makes matter warmer is ___heat___. Heat can be added to an object to raise the object's ___temperature___. Some materials need more ___energy___ to raise their temperature than others.

Name ______________________ TOPIC PRACTICE 4

Heat

Use one of these words to complete sentences 1–7.

thermometer	contracts	energy	temperature
degrees	insulators	expands	

1. The ___temperature___ of an object is a measure of how hot or cold that object is.
2. Matter ___expands___ when it is heated.
3. It takes more ___energy___ to heat water than it takes to heat soil.
4. You can use a(n) ___thermometer___ to measure temperature.
5. Metals are generally not very good ___insulators___ because heat flows through them quickly.
6. When matter is cooled, it ___contracts___, or gets smaller.
7. Temperature is measured in units called ___degrees___.

Answer these questions in your own words.

8. You are going on a camping trip to the North Pole. What materials would you use to make your tent in order to stay warm?
   Answers will vary. Examples are wool, cotton, or goose down, or something with air pockets.
9. An egg is placed in a frying pan. The frying pan is then placed on the stove. How is heat transferred from the stove?
   The heat flows from the stove to the frying pan and then from the frying pan to the egg.

Name ______________________ EXPLORE ACTIVITY 5
Page 1

Investigate What Materials Light Passes Through

Hypothesize What kinds of materials can light pass through? How might you test your ideas?

Write a **Hypothesis:**

Possible hypothesis: Light passes through materials that are not opaque.

Test these materials to see which ones allow light to pass through.

Materials

- flashlight
- large balloon
- classroom materials

Procedures

1. **Experiment** Hold one material at a time in front of the lighted flashlight. Does the light shine through the material? Record your observations.
   The answers depend on the materials selected.
2. **Observe** Blow up your balloon. Look through the balloon. What do you observe now?
   Light passes through the balloon.
3. **Experiment** Try changing the other materials in some way. You may want to fold the papers several times to make them thicker, or crumple up the plastic wrap. After you have made a change in the material, test the material again. Record both the change you made and any new observations.
   The answers will depend on the changes made. Some changes may increase the amount of material the light must pass through, decreasing the amount of light reaching the student. Other changes may have the opposite effect.

Name ______________________ EXPLORE ACTIVITY 5
Investigate What Materials Light Passes Through Page 2

Conclude and Apply

1. **Classify** Which materials did the light pass through? List them. Which materials blocked the light? Make a separate list of the materials.
   The answers depend on the materials tested.
2. **Explain** What was the effect of the change you made to each material?
   Answers will vary. More light would pass through the inflated balloon.

Going Further: Apply

3. **Identify** Look at the list of materials that light passed through. What properties do these materials have in common?
   Possible answer: The materials are thin, clear, or light-colored.

Inquiry

Think of your own questions that you might test. What other materials would you like to test?

My Question Is:
Possible answer: Can light pass through my hand?

How I Can Test It:
Possible answer: Place my hand in front of the flashlight and move it around.

My Results Are:
Possible answer: Light cannot pass through my hand.

Name ______________________ ALTERNATIVE EXPLORE 5

Window Decorations

Materials

- construction materials as in Explore Activity
- tape
- string

Procedures

1. With a partner, plan how you will construct a "stained-glass" decoration to hang in a window. Your decoration must include at least four different materials that allow different amounts of light to pass through them. Be creative in your design. Draw or describe your design on a separate sheet of paper.
2. Use tape to construct your decoration.
3. Use string to hang your decoration in a window.

Conclude and Apply

Explain your choice of materials for your window decoration.

Student's explanations should include a description of the relative amount of light that passes through the materials.

Name ______________________ READING STUDY GUIDE 5
Page 1

Light

Fill in the blanks.

What Does Light Pass Through?

1. Light is a form of **energy**.
2. Light can make **matter** move or change.
3. The Sun, lightning, and fire are all examples of **natural** sources of light.
4. Light travels in **straight lines** from its source.
5. Materials that do not allow any light to pass through them are called **opaque** materials.
6. Opaque materials create **shadows**.
7. Light rays that do not pass through a material **are reflected** from it.
8. Light rays change the **direction** in which they are traveling when they are reflected from a surface.
9. You see an object because light that is reflected from the object enters your **eyes**.
10. Light rays are reflected in many different directions from a rough **surface**.
11. Light rays change direction when they move from one **material** to another.
12. As light rays move from air to water or from water to air, they **bend**.

Name ______________________ READING STUDY GUIDE 5
Light Page 2

Fill in the blanks.

Light Can Change Matter

13. A camera uses **light** to make a photograph.
14. The film inside a camera is coated with **chemicals** that change when light shines on them.
15. Powerful beams of light that can cut steel are called **lasers**.
16. Lasers can read special codes of **information** on items at the supermarket.
17. Plants cannot live and grow without **sunlight**.

Name ______________________________ STUDY AID 5

Light

The drawing shows what happens when light rays move from one material to another. Use the drawing to answer the following questions.

The spoon looks bent because the light rays bend as they pass from one material to another.

1. What solids are shown in the drawing?

A glass and a spoon

2. What liquid is shown in the drawing?

Water

3. List, in order, the kinds of matter that the light rays move through along their path.

Air, glass, water, glass, air

4. Describe how the spoon looks.

The spoon appears to be bent.

5. Do you think the spoon really has this form? Explain your answer.

No. The spoon looks bent because the light rays bend as they move through the glass and water.

Name ______________________________ SKILL BUILDER 5 *Page 1*

Using Variables

Controlling an Experiment

Variables are things in an experiment that can be changed or controlled. For example, suppose you wanted to answer the question: *What affects how light bends in a liquid?* Here are some variables that could be changed:

- the kind of liquid you use
- the size of the container you use
- the position of the object in the liquid

Procedures

1. Compare Take a close look at the containers in the picture. What differences do you see? Describe them below. These differences are variables. List all the variables you can identify on the left side of the table on the next page. The first variable is given.

Possible answer: There are different sizes and shapes of jars, different types and amounts of liquid in the jars, and different objects in different positions in the jars.

Name ______________________________ SKILL BUILDER 5 *Using Variables Page 2*

2. Communicate Complete the table. After you identify as many variables as you can, indicate how you could control each variable.

Possible answer: Use the same size and shape container, the same type and amount of liquid, or the same type of object in the same position.

Variable	Control
Container	use same size and shape of container
Liquid	use same type and amount of liquid
Object	use same type of object in the same position in the container.

Conclude and Apply

Identify Which one variable would you change to see its effect on the bending of light? Why?

Possible answer: Children may mention any one of the variables. They should recognize that only one variable at a time should be changed.

Name ______________________ CLOZE TEST 5

Light

Fill in the blanks.

Light is a form of ___energy___. There are many different sources of light. The Sun, stars, lightning, fire, and some living things are examples of sources of ___natural___ light. Light travels in ___straight___ lines from its source. Light passes through some materials but not through others. Materials that don't allow light to pass through them are ___opaque___. Materials that block light create ___shadows___.

Name ______________________ TOPIC PRACTICE 5

Light

Which of these items are opaque and which are NOT opaque?
Write each item in the correct list.

wood	plastic bottle	plastic wrap	cardboard
tin can	milk carton	plexiglass	brick
water	air		

OPAQUE	NOT OPAQUE
1. wood	6. plastic bottle
2. cardboard	7. plastic wrap
3. tin can	8. plexiglass
4. milk carton	9. water
5. brick	10. air

Answer these questions in your own words.

11. You are on a camping trip, and you have lost your mirror. What other surfaces could you use to see your reflection? What do these surfaces have in common?
    Answers will vary. Examples include still water or any shiny metal surface, such as a frying pan. All of these surfaces are smooth and shiny.

12. Is light a form of energy? What are natural sources of light? What kind of light is made by people?
    Yes, light is a form of energy. Some examples of natural sources of light are the Sun, stars, lightning, and fire. Some examples of light made by people are lightbulbs, flashlights, and candles.

Name ______________________ EXPLORE ACTIVITY 6
Page 1

Investigate What Makes It Light

Hypothesize You often have to put parts together in a certain way for something to work. How can you put a light bulb, wire, and battery together so that the bulb lights? How might you test your ideas?

Write a **Hypothesis:**
Possible hypothesis: The bulb will light if the bulb, battery, and wire are connected.

Test what makes the bulb light by putting the parts together in different ways.

Materials

- D cell
- small light bulb
- 20 cm wire

Procedures

1. **Observe** Look at the bulb, wire, and cell. How do you think you might put these three things together to make the bulb light? Record any ideas you may have.
   Possible answer: Run the wire from the bulb's base to one end of the battery and place the bulb's tip on the other end of the battery.
2. **Experiment** Try to light the bulb. Draw a picture of each set-up that you try on a separate sheet of paper. Record which ones work and which ones don't.
   Encourage children to try different setups using both battery terminals and the base and tip of the bulb.

Conclude and Apply

1. **Identify** How many ways did you find to light the bulb? How many ways did you find that did not light the bulb?
   Possible answers: There are four possible ways to light the bulb.

Name ______________________ EXPLORE ACTIVITY 6
Investigate What Makes It Light Page 2

2. **Compare and Contrast** How were the ways that worked to light the bulb alike? How were they different from the ways that did not work?
   Possible answer: Each successful setup had to connect both ends of the battery, the tip of the light bulb, and the side or base of the bulb. Unsuccessful setups were probably missing one or more of these elements.

Going Further: Apply

3. **Draw Conclusions** How must the bulb, wire, and cell be put together so that the bulb will light?
   Possible answer: The wire must touch both the cell and the bulb. The tip or side of the bulb must touch the end of the cell opposite the wire.

Inquiry

Think of your own questions that you might test. Can you change your setup and still light the bulb?

My Question Is:
Possible question: Students should suggest a different set of connections.

How I Can Test It:
Possible test: Make the suggested connections and see if the bulb lights.

My Results Are:
Possible answer: Either the bulb lit up or it did not, depending on the connections. See the answer to question 3.

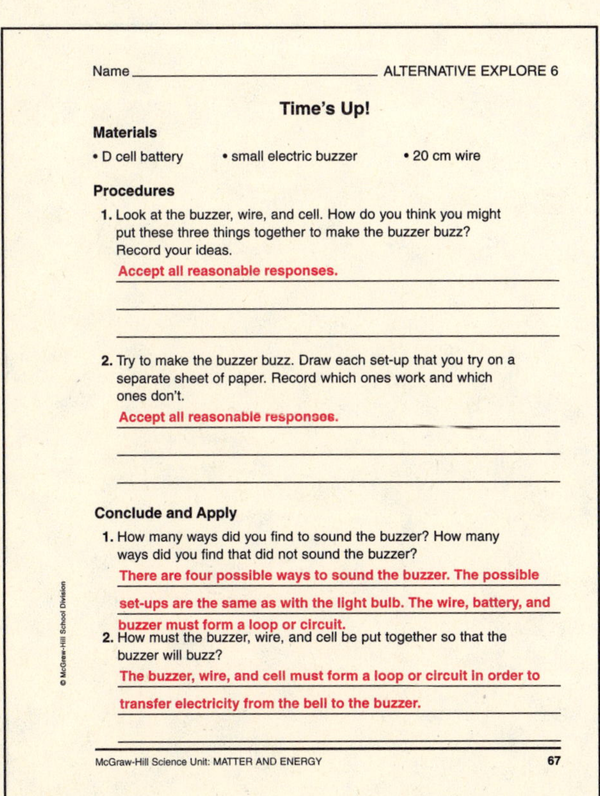

Name ______________________ ALTERNATIVE EXPLORE 6

Time's Up!

Materials

- D cell battery
- small electric buzzer
- 20 cm wire

Procedures

1. Look at the buzzer, wire, and cell. How do you think you might put these three things together to make the buzzer buzz? Record your ideas.

   Accept all reasonable responses.

2. Try to make the buzzer buzz. Draw each set-up that you try on a separate sheet of paper. Record which ones work and which ones don't.

   Accept all reasonable responses.

Conclude and Apply

1. How many ways did you find to sound the buzzer? How many ways did you find that did not sound the buzzer?

   There are four possible ways to sound the buzzer. The possible set-ups are the same as with the light bulb. The wire, battery, and buzzer must form a loop or circuit.

2. How must the buzzer, wire, and cell be put together so that the buzzer will buzz?

   The buzzer, wire, and cell must form a loop or circuit in order to transfer electricity from the bell to the buzzer.

McGraw-Hill Science Unit: MATTER AND ENERGY 67

Name ____________________ READING STUDY GUIDE 6
Page 1

Electricity

Fill in the blanks.

What Makes It Light?

1. A cell is a source of electricity.
2. A group of things that work together is called a(n) system.
3. A bulb, wire, and cell work together as a(n) electrical system.
4. Electricity is a form of energy that travels in a circuit.
5. The path that electricity flows through is called a(n) circuit.
6. A circuit is like a train track.
7. A train needs a complete path to travel on.
8. Electricity will flow through a complete path, which is called a(n) closed circuit.
9. A closed circuit has no gaps.
10. Electricity cannot flow through a(n) open circuit.

How Can You Control the Flow of Electricity?

11. A(n) switch is used to open or close an electric circuit.
12. Pushing a switch one way allows electricity to flow in a complete path.

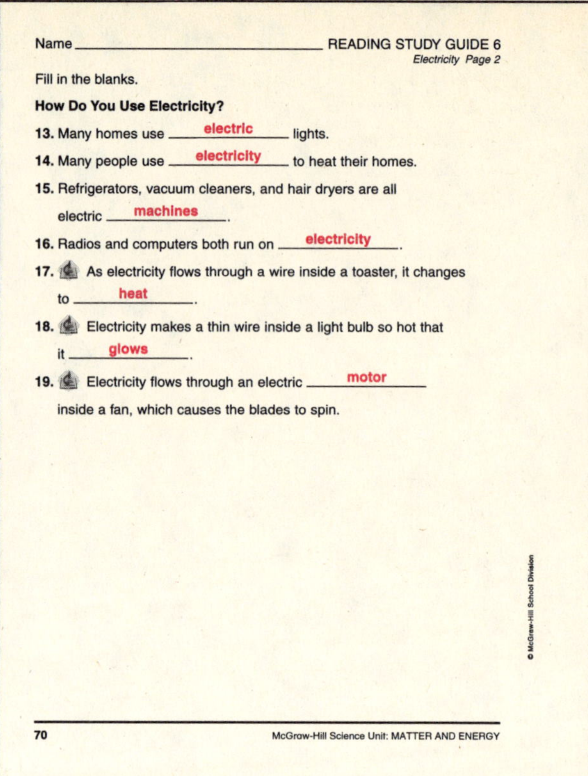

Name ____________________ READING STUDY GUIDE 6
Electricity Page 2

Fill in the blanks.

How Do You Use Electricity?

13. Many homes use electric lights.
14. Many people use electricity to heat their homes.
15. Refrigerators, vacuum cleaners, and hair dryers are all electric machines.
16. Radios and computers both run on electricity.
17. As electricity flows through a wire inside a toaster, it changes to heat.
18. Electricity makes a thin wire inside a light bulb so hot that it glows.
19. Electricity flows through an electric motor inside a fan, which causes the blades to spin.

Name ____________________ STUDY AID 6

Electricity

A chart is a way to organize information. This chart compares open circuits and closed circuits. The left column in the chart compares a circuit to a train track. The right column in the chart describes how electricity flows through a circuit.

Open and Closed Circuits	
(A) A circuit is like a train track. There must be a complete path for the train to travel. GO	Electricity needs a closed circuit, or complete path, to flow. A closed circuit has no gaps. FLOW
(B) If there is a gap in the path, the train won't go. STOP	An open circuit has a gap. Electricity cannot flow through an open circuit. NO FLOW

Use the chart to answer the following questions.

1. How is a circuit like a train track?
   There must be a complete circuit for electricity to flow.
2. What will make a train stop moving along a track?
   A gap or opening in its path
3. What will stop the flow of electricity?
   An opening in the circuit

Name ______ QUICK LAB 6
Page 1

Make a Flashlight

Hypothesize A flashlight is a source of light that uses cells as its source of electricity. How can you put the materials together to make a model of a flashlight?

Write a **Hypothesis:** Possible hypothesis: I can make a flashlight by placing the cells in the paper tube so that opposite ends are touching, then connecting the wire to the bulb and to both cells.

Materials

- 2 D cells
- paper tube
- 30 cm wire
- flashlight bulb

Procedures

Make a Model Use the materials provided for you to construct a model of a flashlight.

Conclude and Apply

1. **Explain** How is your model like a real flashlight? How is your model different?
Possible answer: The model is like a flashlight because it uses cells and a light bulb to produce light. It is different because it does not have a switch.

2. **Communicate** Draw a diagram of your model flashlight's circuit on a separate sheet of paper. How are you able to turn your circuit on and off?
Possible answer: Turn the flashlight on and off by moving the wire or the bulb tip on and off the battery terminals or separating and connecting the cells.

Going Further Electricity can flow through some types of materials but not others. How can you use a circuit to find out whether electricity can flow through certain materials? Write and conduct an experiment.

My Hypothesis Is:
Possible Hypothesis: Electricity can only flow through certain materials.

My Experiment Is:
Possible Experiment: Place a variety of types of materials in the path of the flashlight circuit. See if the bulb lights. Suggested materials are copper wire, aluminum foil, string, plastic cord or paper clip, metal paper clip, and wooden craft stick.

My Results Are:
Answers will vary depending on materials tested. The bulb will light when copper, aluminum foil, and the metal paper clip are placed in the circuit. It will not light when the other materials are in the path.

Name ______ CLOZE TEST 6

Electricity

Fill in the blanks.

You can put together a cell, bulb, and wire to form a(n) system, or group of things that work together. Just like a train set, these parts have to be put together in a certain way for the system to work. These parts form an electrical circuit. Electricity is a form of energy. The source of electricity is the cell. The system uses electrical energy to light the bulb.

Name ______ TOPIC PRACTICE 6

Electricity

Write these words to complete sentences 1–6.

open switch heat circuit closed cell

1. A path that electricity flows through is called a(n) circuit.
2. Electricity changes to heat when it flows through a toaster.
3. Electricity will not flow through a circuit that is open.
4. A device that is used to open or close an electrical circuit is called a(n) switch.
5. You can play your CD player when its electrical circuit is closed.
6. One source of electricity is called a(n) cell.

Answer these questions in your own words.

7. Describe the closed circuit in a flashlight. Is the flashlight on or off when the circuit is closed?
Electricity flows from the cell through the switch to the light bulb and back to the cell. The flashlight is on when the circuit is closed.
8. A storm has caused the electricity in your home to go off. Which items that usually use electricity might still work? Why?
Answers will vary. Examples include battery powered items, such as radios, TVs, CD players, flashlights, and laptop computers. These items will still work because they have alternate sources of electricity (batteries or cells).

Name ______________________________ CHAPTER PRACTICE
Page 1

Energy

Circle the letter of the best answer.

1. Temperature is a measure of

   a. cooked food. **b.** how cold it is.
   (**c.**) how hot or cold something is. **d.** degrees.

2. Heat travels easily through a conductor, but does NOT travel easily through a(n)

   (**a.**) insulator. **b.** thermometer.
   c. solid. **d.** liquid.

3. Heat always flows from warmer objects to

   a. the ground. **b.** hot objects.
   c. plants. (**d.**) cooler objects.

4. Opaque items, which light cannot pass through, create

   a. darkness. (**b.**) shadows.
   c. energy. **d.** matter.

5. Light that does NOT pass through an object

   a. looks white to the human eye. **b.** bends.
   c. creates energy. (**d.**) is reflected off the object.

6. A cell is

   (**a.**) a source of electricity.
   b. a kind of circuit.
   c. a form of energy.
   d. something that opens and closes a circuit.

Name ______________________________ CHAPTER PRACTICE
Energy Page 2

Circle the letter of the best answer.

7. When light rays pass from one material to another, they

   a. disappear. **b.** break.
   (**c.**) bend. **d.** make shadows.

8. The path that electricity follows is called a

   a. cell. (**b.**) circuit.
   c. switch. **d.** light.

9. When matter is heated, it

   (**a.**) expands. **b.** changes form.
   c. changes color. **d.** gets smaller.

10. Which of these items is NOT opaque?

   a. a computer disk (**b.**) a window
   c. a cell **d.** a movie screen

11. Heat is

   a. a measure of temperature. **b.** a mixture.
   c. a form of electricity. (**d.**) a form of energy.

12. A closed circuit

   a. prevents electricity from flowing.
   b. means you have a dead light bulb.
   (**c.**) allows electricity to flow.
   d. makes the temperature rise.